In Search of
the Magic Mushroom

PSILOCYBE MEXICANA

JEREMY SANDFORD

In Search of
the Magic Mushroom

A Journey through Mexico

PETER OWEN · LONDON

ISBN 0 7206 0421 4

PETER OWEN LIMITED
12 Kendrick Mews Kendrick Place London SW7

First British Commonwealth edition 1972
© 1972 Jeremy Sandford

Printed in Great Britain by
Bristol Typesetting Co Ltd
Barton Manor St Philips Bristol 2

CONTENTS

LIST OF ILLUSTRATIONS

ACKNOWLEDGMENTS

The author is grateful for permission to reprint extracts from the following books and articles:

'Amanita Muscaria' by Colin Moorcraft, *Frendz* Magazine

Anahuac by Marc Chadbourne, Elek Books

Common Edible Mushrooms by Clyden Christiansen, University of Minnesota Press

Lectures by R. G. Wasson and Richard Evans Schultes, *The Psychedelic Reader* and *Texas Journal of Pharmacy*, published by permission of University Books Inc., New Hyde Park, New York

'O Magik Mushroom' by Lynn Barnton, *Oz* Magazine

Poisonous Fungi by John Ramsbottom, Penguin Books

The Sacred Mushroom by Andrija Puharich, Victor Gollancz

The Sacred Mushroom and the Cross by John M. Allegro, Hodder & Stoughton

The Teaching of Don Juan: A Yaqui Way of Knowledge by Carlos Castaneda, University of California and Penguin Books: reprinted by permission of the Regents of the University of California

Wayside and Woodland Fungi by W. P. K. Findlay, Frederick Warne

'What the Gods Turned On On' by Robert Graves, *Queen* Magazine

The photographs are reproduced by courtesy of the following:

J. Allan Cash, facing page 129 (bottom)

Camera Press, facing pages 33 (bottom); 64 (top and bottom); 65 (bottom); 97 (top and bottom); 128 (bottom)

John Hillelson/Magnum: photo Henri Cartier-Bresson, facing page 65 (top); photos Wayne Miller, facing page 96 (top and bottom); photo Inge Morath, facing page 128 (top)

Barbara Jackson, facing pages 32 and 129 (top)

Bill MacKenzie, facing page 33 (top, left and right)

Line drawings by Josephine Ranken

In finalising this book, I have drawn on supplementary research by Robin Herbert-Smith and Alan Klein—J.S.

AMANITA MUSCARIA

'One side will make you grow taller, and the other side will make you grow shorter.'

'One side of *what*? The other side of *what*?' *thought* Alice to herself.

'Of the mushroom,' said the Caterpillar. . ; .

ALICE IN WONDERLAND

'El honguillo viene por si mismo no se sabe de donde Como el viento que viene sin saber de donde ni porque.'

MULATEER OF R. GORDON WASSON

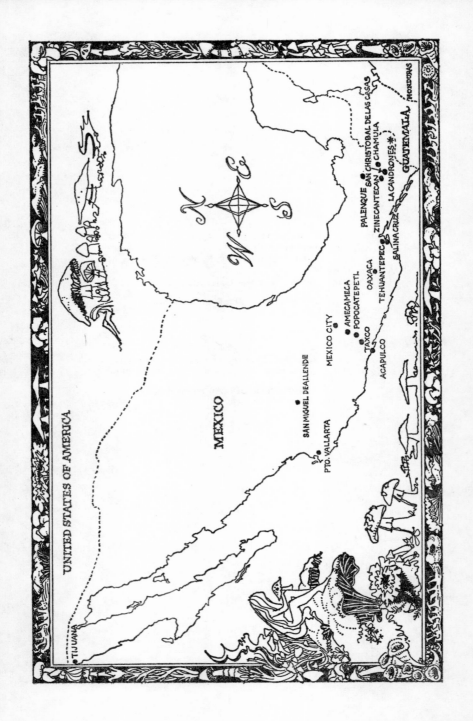

UNITED STATES OF AMERICA

TIJUANA

MEXICO

PTO. VALLARTA

SAN MIGUEL DE ALLENDE

MEXICO CITY
AMECAMECA
POPOCATEPETL
TAXCO
ACAPULCO
OAXACA
TEHUANTEPEC
SALINA CRUZ
LACANDRONES
ZINECANTECAN
CHAMULA
SAN CHRISTOBAL DELAS CASAS
PALENQUE
GUATEMALA
HONDURAS

I

In Search of the Magic Mushroom

In Indian territory, many days' trek from the farthest jeep track, grow the mysterious magic mushrooms of the mountains of Mexico. The hallucinations they excite are of unparalleled beauty, although it is said by some that those who taste them may lose their masculinity. This book tells of my travellings through Mexico and search for the hallucinatory experience.

Quite apart from its mushrooms, I found that Mexico is an exotic country. In Mexico the abnormal is normal, nothing is as you might expect it to be.

I recall a flock of sheep travelling on the roof of a bus.

A Saint that exploded because of the rockets stuffed in him.

A hotel that staggered and rocked in the grip of an earthquake.

Servants in luxury hotels who behaved most oddly. So I shall write of these things also. Often I thought that Britain, affluent, over-standardised, over-predictable, could learn things from Mexico.

A young Mexican choir are travelling with me, lithe girls with flashing eyes and wide pouting lips and young men of great beauty.

As the wheels of the plane first touch the soil of Mexico City with a great thump, one of the choir urges them, 'Three cheers on "OO!"'

And the choir shout 'Ooooooooo!'

'And now on "EE!"'

'Eeeeeeeee!'

'And now on "AH!"'

'Aaaaaaaah!'

'And now on "OH!"'

'Ooooooooh!'

Then we are out on the runway in the stench of the hot steamy night. The lights in various quarters of Mexico City are different in colour – browny-white, copper, bluey-white, white as stars, golden, mellow, some constant and bright, some glimmering like glow-worms.

And behind me the Mexican choir are shouting and applauding. In the plane they almost got out of hand at one point. They were larking about, the men trying on first one and then another of the girls' ornamental hats. They had been doing a tour of Germany and one of the boys had bought a complete outfit of lederhosen which he disappeared into the toilet to try on.

They were moving about so much that there was apparently a danger they would disrupt the balance of the plane. The captain found it necessary at frequent intervals to announce 'Please fasten your safety belts, we are entering an area of turbulence . . . .' in order to keep them quiet.

The Mexican character is exuberant, I found, and this exuberance is also a feature of the country they inhabit. Not so long ago, near Paricutin, a quiet cornfield humped its back and slowly turned into first a mound, then a hillock, then a hill, then a mountain and over the next eighteen months it grew to the astounding height of over 1,700 feet.

Fortunately it then stopped, but the tradition is continued in smaller eruptions all the time, all over Mexico. The Mexican landscape is alive – vibrant and with a living force of its own that I have not seen elsewhere.

Mexicans love home-made fireworks, and let them off on the slightest provocation, especially at fiestas. Also, they love fire-arms. While I was there the crackle of musketry used to shatter the balmy Mexican night. I never heard them ringing the bells of their churches. Instead, the usual idea seemed to be to climb onto the roof or into the campaniles, and go at the bells with hammers and crowbars.

This same quality of exuberance, if that is the word, was in their demonstrations. I was present at that time when thousands of students went surging through the streets, and later were murdered in handfuls by the hated *granaderos* – riot police.

At the same time a few hundred other Mexicans were having their homes razed to the ground by the same *granaderos* because they were on unauthorised land. As if this wasn't enough, in another part of Mexico unexpected floods were resulting in the collapse of hundreds of adobe shacks.

I don't remember the exoticism of Mexico, though, only as violent and explosive. I remember a flower strewn balcony in the little hill town of Taxco. And a posada in San Miguel de Allende, just a blank door in a wall facing a long narrow street. I banged on the door and it was opened by an ill-smelling man in an ancient hat, faded jeans and dirty shirt, who had been sleeping on a blanket on the floor just inside. I went in and he led me through the darkness of a courtyard totally filled with riotous vegetation. At the end was a low archway, and we passed fetid smelling latrines, stall-like erections of brick covered with bits of plaster, with flapping ill-hinged stable-like doors and a steady stream of water oozing out underneath them. No, this was the wrong way. We returned into the courtyard and to a cell-like apartment, a room containing a couple of black tin beds with rough mattresses, faded coarse sheets and one tatty blanket apiece. There was no furnishing in the whitewashed room but a crucifix, and a shelf hanging down from two pieces of string. The floor was made of tiles. There was a light bulb hanging from the ceiling, but it didn't work.

The doors wouldn't lock. Anyway, as it was so hot I left them open. I peeled off my jeans and put them under the pillow. It's in my jeans pocket that I keep my money. In the middle of the night I woke up to see a man standing in the darkness in the middle of the room, staring at me intently. Realising that I was awake he said he was sorry, he was looking for a friend. He went out hastily.

The next thing that happened was the birds. Long before it was light there were sundry chirpings and chirrupings from amongst the foliage outside. And now as light began to filter down through the dense arms of the leaves, the hotel broke out into a veritable chorus of birds. Looking out from the door of my cell I saw that the whole of the inner patio had been made into a sort of cage, and was totally filled with birds, some softly chirruping, others loudly vociferating, and I sank back to sleep again overwhelmed by such exuberance.

They make use of ninety-two different types of chilli. Their cuisine is said to be the oldest in the world. The second oldest is Chinese, but the most recent is French which I am told we use in a modified form in Britain. Mexican cuisine dates from the early Mayan culture over eighteen thousand years ago. From Mexico,

Europe was introduced for the first time to tomatoes, beans, vanilla, chillis, maize, avocados, egg plant, potatoes, peanuts, pumpkins and chocolate, not to mention tobacco.

Prisons in Mexico are often open to the road. One passes a door that is filled with bars, and behind it languishes the prisoner. He peers out, shaggy faced, unshaven, imploring the gift of a coin or food with toothless pink gums and cracked pink lips. His friends and relatives can bring him things to eat, and stand by the door talking to him. When I hand him a coin he curses quietly.

Human excrement is used in the cultivation of vegetables, and one result of this, so Gringos (visiting Americans) told me, is that they are often full of somewhat noxious germs, against which non-Mexicans have little defence.

Later I was to spend many days slowly tossing on a bed locked in the forgotten recesses of some strange illness that kept me pinioned below my sheets but that, curiously, kept me more happy than miserable, lost in a strange euphoric dream, born perhaps of the lethargy of the tropics, that dreamless sleep that is engendered by a heat so intense that there is no room for tension or neurosis, only perhaps melancholy. Except that the word melancholy too seems wrong in such heat, one connects it more with the mists of the British winter afternoon, when children come back for crumpets at tea, rather than with the tropics.

There is an insubstantial feeling throughout the whole of Mexico. Mexico City, a vast modern savage city of many millions of people complete with skyscrapers and mile on mile of gaudily painted one-room concrete wooden or mud-brick huts, used to stand on a lake. The waters have been drained away now but still the city stands on a cushion of mud. When lorries pass you can feel a quivering in the streets beneath your feet. One building, the heavily decorated pretentious marble Opera House, is slowly sinking into the mud and is now five feet lower than it should be. Some say they wish it would vanish completely. Across the road a bank has been acting as a counter-weight, steadily rising. It is now five feet higher than it should be.

Jimmy Nicol is an Englishman who has made his home in Mexico City. He plays in one of the gaudy discotheques. Self-styled 'Fifth Beatle', he stood in for Ringo on drums for six weeks on a

world tour – Ringo was sick. After such an experience, there could
only be Mexico.

'*Jimmie Nicol! El quinto Beatle!*' scream the illuminated letters
above the Champagne a Go-Go.

If the Mexicans have heard of Britain at all it is as the home of
the Beatles. 'Ah, you come from England, the country of Los Beatles
y Los Rolling Stones!' The next question is, how far do you live
from the fabulous city of Liverpool?

Speaking from the heart of the Zona Rosa, an area richer than
our Bond Street, Jimmy told me; 'I get many vibrations from
Mexico. I can't explain it, it's like a magical land, one can do
anything here that you want to if you have a will to do it.

'I've been here a year and a half and I can't get away from it,
this country has something I haven't found in a third of the world,
I call it feeling.

'British people are afraid to talk on trains and buses. Mexicans
are not, they talk with anybody, if they don't like something they
say they don't like it, if they like it they go mad about it.

'It's an exotic country.'

Wild as well as exotic. Towering mountains alternate with vast
expanses of plains. The magnificent sweep of the high country gives
way to ravines which plunge down to the steamy depths of tropical
jungles which have never been explored, with idyllic tropical
beaches where the blue water laps gently and it's far too hot.

Mexico is eight times as large as Britain and has rather fewer
people – forty-seven million. Only one-fifth is suitable for farming.
One can scarcely put a foot down except on the remains of some
ancient civilisation – Mayan, Aztec, or of the later colonisation by
the Spanish.

Mexicans claim that the country invaded by Cortes was more
civilised than the Spain he came from. Official policy is to decry
Spanish customs and get back to the lovely innocence of pre-Spanish
culture, although no one, as far as I know, has yet suggested reviving
the cultural habit of human sacrifice.

In fact, Mexico presents a fascinating counterpoint between the
Spanish tradition, represented by barley-sugar churches, the Spanish
language, richly gilded caskets containing bloody saints and other
horrors, bullfights and horses, and the Indian tradition of exuberance, secretness, joy, polygamy. There are still millions who speak
no Spanish but, rather, a conglomeration of Indian dialects. The

central administration has no way of communicating with them.

Mexico's sadness is it's poverty. Although it is the most prosperous country south of the United States, most families exist in one-room shacks and many never taste meat. Soft drink advertisements sometimes have pictures of luscious steaks where we would have luscious girls.

A cellar at Guanajuato has a museum of human deformity – dwarfs, hunchbacks, Siamese twins, syphilitics, all neatly arranged in mummified rows.

And, since the first rising against the Spanish in the early nineteenth century, there have been at least twelve revolutions.

'Some once idealistic leader grows bombastic, makes himself enemies, forgets his ideals', so writes Marc Chadourne, 'and then in a moment there are guns blasting off, bombs exploding, and trees in the country once more bear their tragic burden of human corpses. Then a new heroic leader comes in and all is the same again.'

This is a country, I found, that alternates between contagious joy and masochistic horror.

2

Careless Talk, Man

'Hi man!'

I am sitting in one of the Mexico City parks in the dusk, and a dark young man with an attractive face comes and sits on the wrought iron seat beside me.

He claps his hands sharply at girls who go past, shouting; *'Pero! Que linda estas!'* 'Great! How pretty you are!'

And the girls look back over their shoulders at us, haughtily.

Then suddenly he turns to me and asks; 'Man, want some grass?'

'Why, have you grass for sale?'

He claps his hand over his mouth.

'Careless talk, man! Man, better be careful! Talk of grass! If they find it here on me, much trouble. Much much trouble.'

A boy joins us on the wrought iron seat. About twelve, his face is beautiful with the grave, high-cheek boned, slope-forehead features of the true Indian.

He carries with him a red leather box, covered with brass studs, containing shoe-cleaning gear. No sooner has the boy sat down beside us but a grey-suited man with thick glass spectacles comes and sits beside *him* and ask for a shine.

The young man who first spoke whispers behind his hand, while pretending to pick his nose, 'Careful, man. Everyone here talk English.'

Then he says out loud, 'I be in Acapulco. All over. Have many Gringo friends. Have one in Philadelphia, one in Phoenix, you know.'

When the shoe-shining is complete, and the grey-suited man has gone, he says conspiratorily, 'That man was a policeman, he want to know why I talk to you.'

He turns to the shoe-cleaning boy and says a few words to him in Indian, not Spanish. Then he says to me, 'This genuine Indios Mayan boy who be on the beach at Acapulco as well, man. He have many many friends in the States. See many people. Yes man. Genuine Indios, from Yucatan. You like him?'

The little boy smiles at me.

He asks again, 'You like him?'

'Well, yes,' I say.

'Like a lot? Mucho?'

At this point, the little boy abruptly pulls a tape measure from the pocket of his leather trousers. One of those small circular steel ones. Pointing between his legs he says, in unexpectedly good English, 'Eighteen centimetres! Mucho! Poof! Very mucho! You like to see?'

He taps me on the knee and mutters behind his hand, 'One hundred pesos!'

The last buses, brightly illumined, carrying on their front antique Indian names, Anahuac, Tepotlan, Aculotenco, Ahuehueten, and also Satellite (this last a new housing project), are surging past out of Mexico City, away.

It is cooler now in the night. Soon I leave the plushy blocks of the Zona Rosa, and walk along poorer streets.

I pass shops selling pulque (a white alcoholic drink), tacos, tortillas, plastic shoes, belts, rare stones, melons, passion fruit, pumpkins, everything conceivable in brightly lit little caverns.

In between the caverns there are alleyways guarded by gaudy shrines, off which open long lines of one-roomed little houses. Most of the houses are little more than shacks made only of crazy filthy planks stuck together, roofed with corrugated iron and sometimes old blankets or newspapers have been laid across the iron to make them more waterproof.

The street is crowded with people. I see a little dark-haired girl in a pretty dress lying in the middle of the street, peering down a dark drain in amazement. A little further on and there is a vast eight foot hole in the middle of the pavement, without warning.

A mother asks me for 'one peso'. By her on the pavement a child lies writhing, apparently in agony.

Large silver studs have been put across the road to stop the traffic going too fast. They are the size of motor wheel hubs. Over them lurches an occasional ancient huge American car filled with young Mexicans. Many of these cars have curtained windows or are painted with flowers or other gaudy designs.

I mingle with the crowd assembled on the pavement where an attractive girl lies on her back, flat out. Drunk? Dead? I look up her skirts, up her stiff thighs. I look through a door into one of the better class courtyards, where, illumined by a brilliant green luminous effigy of Christ, young men and girls dance, the girls beautiful in white frilly muslin.

I hear a child screaming, and, looking through a window, see her father whipping her savagely with a belt. Through the window of another of these little houses I see a tiny room, a vast bed with purple coverings, a candle burning in front of a crucifix and a couple of family portraits, a gaudy calendar, some pink curtains, a vast looking-glass, and an old granny dressed in shawl, apron, and plimsolls, fingering through the hair of a little girl for nits.

There is never silence in these parts. The throaty roar of buses, the blare of television, the crackle of radio. 'Man is a weed in these regions.'

Whole families are sitting out in the street, eating their evening meal in the hot night at rough tables, sitting on chairs, oil cans, boxes.

I see young Indian girls, perhaps thirteen years old, wandering through the streets, barefoot, a look of despair on their faces, and in their arms, their children – children in the arms of children.

I see all the innumerable varieties of beggars, the halt and the maimed that in Britain we shut up, here at large, trying to scrape a few pesos together. And though their life is one of horror, they are at any rate, unlike our British maimed, still in touch with society.

A huge Ford passes, with a stunningly beautiful girl at the wheel, her wool jersey cut low round her pretty breasts, between which nestles a piece of expensive jewellery.

The hotels here are vast and beautiful as they stretch into the sky, with a romance of their own. The shopping centre, the cafes, the restaurants have more style than anything in London.

And here are the same pathetic Indian beggars and desperate children giving it the lie. As I sit in a bar a beggar thrusts beneath my nose small marble statues of naked women.

Another man comes with his threadbare son into the cafe where

I am drinking coffee, points appealingly at the ornamental cakes that lie on the table, placed there temptingly for me by the management.

'Please, please,' he cries, and finally I give him one of these brief cream-covered little pasties, as if a cake might solve the poverty of millions.

Some of those who stroll through these plush and idyllic regions, these broad avenues linked by statues and fringed with pines, bounded by the vast shiny stories of fabulous hotels, may feel that Mexico City is a cruel and materialistic and capitalistic city, home of the very rich and the very poor, home of the unmarried wealthy playboy flitting from suite to suite and girl to girl, a bitter contrast to the unmarried penniless young mother, herself no more than a child, begging in the gutter, hoping for one peso.

In some ways, Mexico City today seems less like a revolutionary capital than like that fabled almost feudal city that the Emperor Maximilian ruled in fabulous splendour for only two years before his murder, in the 1870s. Elegant Parisian ladies wandered then through Chapultepec Park and the Emperor's wife was able to watch him driving to work down a long avenue from her window in the ornamental castle built on the hill.

Blowing your car horn in Mexican cities is illegal. There is a fine of fifty pesos, about ten pounds, for an ordinary blow, and a fine four times as large for a particularly offensive rhythm known in America as Get a Shave and a Hair Cut. Despite this, the streets of Mexico are made hideous with horn blowing. In a group of cars it is impossible for the police to tell which one has blown his horn.

There are also wolf-whistle horn calls and even the sound of an elk on heat can be heard emerging amidst these prosaic surroundings and ordinary strident horn blasts, amongst cars raring to go in traffic jams in the wide streets of the opulent quarters round Hamburgo and Reforma and Insurgentes.

The sheer blazing intensity of life here, and the lack of that sort of inhibition which so often makes us in Britain view splendid gestures with a depreciatory and embarrassed air, can nowhere better be seen than in the way that the Mexicans fill their public places with mosaic, statues, and other splendid devices.

The park of Alameda is dominated, through the gentle forms of the trees, by a vast thirty foot high moving screen lit up with three thousand golden bulbs depicting Flamenco dancers, and donkeys, paid for by Coca-cola.

Mexicans say that whereas the New York subway stations are filled with advertising posters and graffiti, *their* metro is decorated with modern paintings and sculptures. One station has a high relief mural in copperplate entitled simply 'El Hombre'. This mural measures thirty-one feet long and nine feet high. Other murals depict 'Man and Woman', and 'Themes of Birth and Maternity'. Across the entrance to the subway a second mural of similar size will depict the 'Development of Man towards Form, Conscience and Spiritual Projection'. This station, San Lazaro, will also have two triangular stained glass windows, one of them fifty-nine feet long and twenty-two feet high depicting 'Man before Chaos'. The other window will have two male and two female figures representing tranquility.

It was from the grass-seller and his friend from Yucatan that I first heard of the magic mushroom.

'Oh yes,' the grass-seller said, 'the hallucinations it gives are indeed of unparalleled beauty.'

'Tell me, where do they grow?' I asked. 'And how can I get to them?'

The directions he gave me were complicated. It seemed that you must go during the rainy season to a certain little town, change buses and then continue by second-class bus to another town, then on again until you reached, on foot, a town far away in the midst of the mountains. I resolved to taste the magic mushrooms.

'The hippies here have been thrown out from their shanties beside Lake Chappalla,' a *mestizo* told me.

'I didn't know there *were* any hippies in shanties by Lake Chappalla?'

'Oh yes, a lot. You know, hippies. Hippies Americanos.'

'Why were they thrown out?'

'They were wandering around the town, without their clothes on. In a state of undress. And they were smoking marijuana. And eating the magic mushrooms.'

'The magic mushrooms! Good! Tell me where I can find them! Where are they? Would they have any for me?'

'Oh no, I don't suppose so.'

From a member of the American drop-out I learned more about the magic mushrooms, and his account of them whetted my appetite for these strange fungi.

'You get them in this mountain town that is filled with people, and lousy with men wandering round muttering, *"Hongos magicos, precios realisticos."* "Magic mushrooms at realistic prices." '

'People say they reveal to you the source of troubles as yet unknown and also unknown illnesses. If you feel weak and debilitated the magic mushrooms will reveal the exact place of the debilitation through a sort of throbbing as if a bright light surrounded it, like a halo.'

My informant brushed a piece of earth from his dazzling white clothes. 'You eat the mushrooms in small pieces. I was given them by an Indian from whom I bought a palapa, deep in the jungle. I still return occasionally.

'The atmosphere in the town where you buy them is happy and relaxed, due perhaps to the number of people who consume the magic mushrooms. You prepare them by cutting them up into little pieces and pouring hot water over them. Then you eat the morsels.

'They say that women become sexually excited by the mushrooms, but that men may become generally debilitated so that they are no longer able to perform.

'It is important to lie on the floor before you start. This is because the initial effect of the magic mushrooms is powerful – the effect on the system has been compared to the powerful thrust of a plane taking off.

'There are two prices for the mushrooms. One, the cheap price, is for those who are genuine searchers after mystical truth. The other, more pricey, is for those who are taking the mushrooms for kicks.

'The experience of the magic mushrooms is timeless – you take leave of all sensations of time. And this is interesting because the local Indians are conspicuous for their lack of any sense of time. There are notices in the town in their language giving details of fiestas that are going to take place, that sort of thing. Everything is in Indian until you come to the time when it is going to take place. That is written in Spanish because the Indians mostly have no words for time.'

'But what is the experience of taking mushrooms like?' I ask
him.

'Like nothing on earth. What a pity. Usually I have a few pieces
of the magic mushrooms in my pocket. But I've run out now till
the next rainy season.'

3

Girls

Girls . . . high breasted, live, with flashing eyes, Mexican girls are often beautiful. Dressing is easy for them, since in many places the temperate climate allows them to wear the same summer dress all the year. In Puerto Vallarda on the Pacific, for instance, most of the girls have only one cotton dress, tight-waisted, with a flared skirt, and they wear this all the time except when they retire to the river that runs down a gorge through the middle of town, where, in their hundreds, they go for their weekly wash.

On the shores of this meandering river there are innumerable little shelters constructed from bamboos and palms, twisted exotically into the shape of little wigwams or tents. The girls kneel beneath these awnings and remove their dresses and scrub away at them with a couple of stones and a bit of soap.

The houses which line the ravine have mainly now been bought by Gringos, and much pleasure is given to them as they sit sipping their cocktails on those lofty terraces above, for they can look down into the ravines and see the beautiful naked girls washing their clothes.

Mexican girls, I found, are often extremely coquettish, eyeing passers-by in the street with flashing delight in a way that they don't do in Britain. It may be that the reason for this joyful coquettishness is that the customs for the middle classes are strict, and hence provide a certain security for the girls.

A man tells me, 'They have a fantastic respect for virginity here. It's immensely important to them that the girl they marry should be a virgin. For instance, I remember how one night I was making love with a Mexican girl, and when we'd finished she said to me, "Now turn back the covers, look at the sheets, and be proud of yourself". I turned back the sheets and saw there was a

lot of blood on them. The girl was intensely proud that she was a
virgin. But was she really a virgin? I don't think she was telling
me the truth, I think she was just being clever and tricked me.
And, oh God, why do they have to do that sort of thing? It makes
me sick! It's such a waste of energy and time that they should have
to practise such deception.

'However, tight-laced though they may be, there is also a sort
of joy about the middle-class Mexican girls. When I slept with
another girl, whose name was Maria, it was Saturday night, and
the following morning as the church bells began to ring, she
jumped from bed and said, "Quick, quick, I must go to Mass!"
I said, "No! Stay here! Why do you have to go? Why do you feel
that you have to go and confess?" She said, "I'm not going to
confess, but to give thanks for a very beautiful act." '

One day when I am travelling in a taxi with an attractive
American girl, two Mexican boys who are also in the taxi get
talking to us. Realising that she doesn't understand much Mexican,
they ask whether I will swap her for two Mexican girls. The situation is odd, and it becomes even stranger when the taxi, apparently
running perfectly all right, suddenly breaks down and the driver
gets out and starts looking in the engine. The boys promptly pay
the very high sum which he has demanded from us. 'But it's quite
all right, they will find us another taxi.'

As we're walking down the street, they make various attempts to
detach the girl from me. If I hadn't hung on to her arm as hard
as I could they may well have succeeded. And then what would
have happened? Who knows?

Mexican boys often ask with a sort of breathless fear about the
relationship between visiting Americans and their girls. It hurts
them, I think, so much happiness. Sometimes they ask, with a sort
of painful fear, 'How many women do you have?' And, if you ask
them the same question in return, they reply, in pain, looking
away, 'Yes, I have two or three'.

Some Mexican men, it seemed to me, take on new girls, new
families, as men in our society buy new cars. Often there is the
main establishment where a man keeps his first wife, his children,
his animals. Then there will be the Casa Chica, the little house,
a small shack, for his girlfriend and her children. And for other
girlfriends, other shacks. One quarter of all babies born in Mexico
are illegitimate.

Passions run high, pride runs high, and sometimes love affairs end in shooting. Because of this, unmarried girls are carefully guarded.

A girl told me, 'I can't go to the cinema with my boyfriend without a chaperone. Wherever we go, mother has to come too. Last night in the car on the way home, I was tired, and I put my head on my boyfriend's shoulder. Mother said, "No, you can't do that till you're married," and she separated us and sat between us.'

A title for a song that might sell well in Mexico would be 'Gringo Girl'. For some Mexican boys get fatally hooked on the Gringo woman, and that is sad for them.

A Gringo girl said, 'The men make your life a curse. Finally I thought I'd found a nice one. We were in a taxi and he was explaining how much we should pay and how we should get to certain places. And even he, as he was getting out, suddenly pinched me between the legs.'

I was drawing some pictures of bulls at one of the bull-rearing studs and a group of Mexican girls gathered round. Then one of the girls seized my pencil, and in the midst of the bulls drew a detailed picture of a carnation. Turning to me, gravely she said, 'Carnation is for passion.'

It is said that marriage between Mexican girls and the visiting white men seldom work. Middle-aged Americans who have gone there to retire, young American drop-outs, American business men there on a visit – many of these are enchanted by the frolicsome and lovely Mexican girls. For her part, a girl who has never had running water or a television, let alone a car and a house with a tiled courtyard and a fountain, may be fooled by the proliferation of these material things into thinking that she loves the visiting Gringo.

One can see them, these sad couples, on the beaches of the various tourist resorts. Sitting in the sun with their Gringo husbands, they all too often feel frustrated and bored. The trouble is that they get ostracised from their own people. It's not so much that the Mexicans don't want to be friendly to them, but that their way of life has become so different that they no longer have a great deal in common. The Gringo husbands often ultimately get bored with them, perhaps because of the difference in cultures.

The saddest story that was told me concerned a girl who had married a Gringo and a few weeks after her marriage he met a

Gringo model girl nearly twice her age, and abandoned her. Divorce is hard to get in Mexico, and so the girl returned to her parents. But, now that she was married, it would be unlikely that she would ever find herself another husband.

One morning I was sitting in a bar in Mexico City, drinking tequila, and at the end of the mahogany-decked bar, there was a man struggling to open the ornate entrance to the gentlemen's toilet, prominently marked 'Senores'. However hard he tried, he didn't seem to be able to get it open. He went on and on, battling with it, shaking it frantically.

Suddenly the door did swing open, but with such force that the man was hurled backwards. Inside the door a vast woman appeared, angrily shaking, shouting, reinforcing what she said with wild gestures and blows from the side of her hand. Mexico is a revolutionary country. But I doubt whether even there a revolution would extend to the occupation by ladies of the gentlemen's toilet.

Mexican children, possessed of exceptional beauty, are loved, cosseted and worshipped by their families. And, in spite of liberal handouts of contraceptives, are still coming into the world at the rate of a million a year. Many pass their first year or so tied to their mothers' backs. However great the poverty of their families, they nearly always live as the centre of an adoring crowd of mothers, aunts, brothers and sisters. And there is seldom silence, seldom loneliness in the Mexican one and two-roomed shacks.

This is all good. But it struck me that there is also another side to the irresponsible and happy-go-lucky attitude of the Mexicans. It struck me that Mexican males may be the victims of a collective Oedipus complex – not in that they wish to murder their fathers but because they desire passionately to marry their mothers and that all women should be their mothers. Often it seemed to me that their attitude to women is brutal, possessive, exploitive, infantile-sexual.

'Look at me, Mummy!' they cry as they lay their women, spawn children, fight for them, make passionate love to them, fire guns, play the trumpet, and finally abandon them with the same cry of 'Look at me, Mummy!'

There are some who would claim that they desire and yet fear women. And that they hate American tourist girls for their detachment, their self-possession, their apparent availability.

While I was there an American girl walked out along the beach after a row with her boyfriend. It seems that she was picked up by the police. She was found dead next morning on that same beach. Every orifice in her body had been stuffed full of sand.

4

An Earthquake

I am sitting in a bus station on the outskirts of Mexico City. It
is a huge room, stuffed with Indians, Indian women carrying
squalling children, ancient Indians carrying livestock, flash young
Indians with all types and shapes and sizes of cardboard boxes
tied up with string. Splendid buses, dramatic, are drawn up in the
next room and have Indian names written on their sides, Tacabaya,
Anahuac.

Just beyond a corrugated iron fence is a huge notice, *Autos
Usados*, 'Used Motors', and the trees beside the road, those dusty
dry parched trees, are hanging with the innumerable dismembered
parts of motor cars which the garage is selling, like some lush
mechanical fruit. Ahead, a hotel has the sign *Cerado* over its door –
it was closed by the police.

The night life in Mexico is very dull now, a Gringo man is telling me. Leaning towards me along the bus station seat he says
there are no whores now, only dancing girls whom you pay to dance
with. As you dance you'll see that their dress falls down and down
over their breasts till it reaches their nipples, almost all of their
breast is exposed. Just at that moment the dance comes to an end,
they hoik their dress up again so you have to pay for another one
in the hope that you may see a bit more. This is for Gringos and
foreigners. For the Mexican it's as exotic as ever, so I'm told.

The Hotel Blitz is built in the shape of an ocean liner, the long
streamlined lines of its windows culminating in a rounded prow.
This modernistic impression is marred, however, by the fact that
half of the Hotel Blitz is in ruins – no glass in the windows, the
gashes of steel girders, some men actually at work either recon-

structing or dismantling it, I can't quite make out which.

One morning, while lying in bed, suddenly I experience the most violent lurching. It feels like the worst sort of hangover, reminiscent of those occasions when one staggers into bed high and the world reels.

Looking out of my window I see that stones which have been attached by hawsers to pieces of wood which hang down from the roof of the building are careering backwards and forwards, crashing heavily into the walls. I open the door and am confronted in the passage with hurrying Americans. 'What's going on?' I ask.

'I don't know, and I'm not staying to find out.'

I run down into the street. This is filled with people gesticulating and shouting. Builders at work on the new underground opposite have stopped work and are standing, laughing as if at a comedy act, as they see our hotel dancing up and down in the grip of its personal earthquake.

The hotel is still rising and falling as I cross the street. The stones fixed to the hawsers continue to clang gently against its walls. I stay there awhile watching the mysterious dance of the hotel, as if it was some street performer. Later, I learn that two people were crushed to death in this earthquake, by the falling top of a concrete garage down the road.

You can't escape from the constant presence of reality. Bells clang and bash throughout the night. It's a dangerous country. Guns go off. Cars drive at you. The earth shakes. Electric wires run bare to the sky, and often collapse in rain, sparking wildly, or topple in earthquakes.

Children will play ball against the walls of some provincial cathedral, and, unlike England, no stuffy verger drives them out with his hideous odour of sanctity. The texture of reality is constantly reaffirmed and shattered by vociferous clangs of bells of many sizes being enthusiastically struck by solitary enthusiasts through the empty watches of the night.

This love of noise has, I think, always been a feature of Mexico. Bernal Diaz, who travelled with Cortes, says, 'As we were retreating we heard the sound of trumpets and also a drum, a most dismal sound indeed it was like an instrument of demons, it resounded so that one could hear it two leagues off. . . . At that moment . . . they were offering the hearts of ten of our comrades and much blood to the idols.'

Some drums are said to be so valuable and sacred that they are always kept on a lead like a dog. And you can do what you like.

Do you want to drink in a pub at any hour of the day? You can. Do you want to start up a little alfresco pub by putting a few bottles in a wheelbarrow and selling to passers-by on a station platform? You can.

Feeling tired? If you want to wrap up in a blanket and sleep on the station platform, you can. Also, should you want to send out your six-year-old boy to sell holy fakes or clean shoes and earn a few pence, so you can drink in the cantina, you can do this also. Always, at the back of it all, I felt a fierce basis of violence.

The British owner of a papier mâché factory in the town of San Miguel di Allende told me, 'People often envy the freedom of the Mexicans, their absence of restrictions. But when you've seen, as I have, a man hit by a taxi six feet into the air in a crowded street and come down clonk! And no one did anything about it, he just lay there for ten, twenty, thirty minutes, then you understand the other side of the picture : this could be called a country without compassion.'

Traffic in Mexico City. The taxis with their emblazoned shark's teeth drive in a way that is terrifying even if you're in them. Hitchhikers may be humiliated by triumphant drivers of cars making slit-throat signs at them, teasing them by slowing down as if to stop for them, and then, as they run for the car, driving on again. Cars filled with young Mexicans even try to run down pedestrians on occasion, emitting eerie screams.

Ordinary people can be rung and offered protection – protection against what? Well, anything that might happen. One may receive a telephone call offering protection perhaps for as little as ten or fifteen pounds a year. 'If you're ever involved in an accident, we have friends at the police station, we will ring up first, pay bail for you, see that you're treated right. We have a hundred lawyers – lawyers attached to the police stations.'

Yes, but protection against what?

'Well, anything that might happen.'

The tale was being told while I was there of a wealthy Vera Cruz businessman who had just been seized by the police and accused of a curious method of getting hold of two million pesos. He took out life insurances on himself amounting to this sum, and then invited out for a trip two of the men he employed in the prosperous saloons and stores that he ran in Vera Cruz.

They had not driven very far, however, when, so it was alleged, he suddenly set upon them and killed them in a lonely spot between Coatzacoalcos and Laguna de Catemaco. How, single-handed, he managed to murder them both has not yet emerged. But, thereafter, it appears that he put their bodies in his car, set it on fire, and pushed it over a ravine.

He then made his secret way to Mexico City and had his face altered, through plastic surgery, out of all recognition. Meanwhile his wife went to pick up the insurance claiming that it was he who had perished in the blazing motor in the ravine near Coatzacoalcos.

A certain Roderigas, knowing that his friend Corella was running for a local authority position in Mexicali on the slogan of 'Let's make Mexicali a clean city', is said to have thought that it would be a good idea to give positive proof of this necessity by secretly bribing the garbage collectors to stop work. Slowly the garbage mounted in Mexicali, but so did Corella's promises that, should he become their representative, he would clean it up.

Another story circulating when I was there concerned a medical student who, at a lesson in surgery, suddenly, as he raised his scalpel preparing to make the first incision in the corpse they were practising on, cried, with horror and amazement, 'Mother!'

It appears that he had recognised the face of his mother, buried four years before, and, as a result of this, later made many allegations that body snatching on a major scale was in vogue in Mexico in order to supply Mexican medical schools with cadavers. However, the truth will always, like so much, remain buried in obscurity. Later there were many to say that it had not been his mother at all.

Amidst the beauty of its parks amongst whose trees gold and marble statues can be seen, and where, in the El Alameda park, strange pillars made of tiles bare their tops, it is easy to forget that there is a more violent and corrupt side to Mexico. But, outside the Banco Aztec, the Banco de Londres y Mexico, and all the vast array of banks that stand near the centre of this town, are uniformed policemen.

People still die in the streets, children still sleep in the streets. Cities are regularly flooded and this is often followed by the wholesale collapse of adobe houses into the mud they were made from.

In 1935 the State seized all foreign investments, including British

The author questions a
local resident

A typical Mexican bus

Indians and Mestizzos

oil. Now Mexico is said to 'float' to a large extent on American capital. The economy is increasing fast (at 6.5 per cent per annum). A new school is built every two hours, and in many areas, such is the thirst for education, these schools are used in shifts. People ask me whether I think there will be yet one more revolution. I say, No.

There are many injustices in Mexico, there are men and women and children who wander through that idyllic country with fear and horror and death written on their faces. In their whole lives they never can own as much money as one man spends in one night at the Acapulco Hilton. But, as a whole – Mexico is getting rich now. They have money coming in – American money. And those who control the tanks and guns are not those who are starving.

Chapultepec Park on a Sunday. Old Indians are wandering round with their blankets neatly folded under their arms. Myriad women are wandering barefoot through the lush grass which is kept green by countless sprays and fountains. And here there is a barrel-organist playing a theme from Verdi, his organ supported on a tall stick. Every few bars the man moves it across the green grass.

Between the people, statues stand beneath tall trees, and there are fountains sprinkling up water and golden women wandering about in the shallow lakes that lie amid the verdure, the water reaching up to the level of their thighs. Innumerable salesmen wander through the park, selling beautiful nothings of silver paper and coloured whirligigs, a fantastic variety of brightly coloured gas-filled balloons in great clusters, each with a paper cap on its head and painted in orange, purples, all the vivid colours of the rainbow.

Here is a woman with further supplies of these same gas balloons, carrying with her a vast transparent red balloon containing more gas to fill them with. Other men run round carrying small trays on which are innumerable types of jellies. A little further on a band concert is in progress, the gleaming brassy bowls of five sousaphones raised triumphantly and observantly into the sky. And everywhere wander Indians, wonderful men with their blankets neatly rolled hanging at their waists, and their women folk so beautiful, their faces innocent and bland like ponies.

B

At the entrance to this park, where the roads fork to either side, there is a vast thirty-foot-high statue of the Goddess Diana which, it is said, has caused one hundred accidents because the shape of the woman is so lovely that people drive off the road.

Here is an incredible church, a wonderful Spanish confection, lit up all over its sugar-candy pillars and decorations by myriad low-voltage bulbs that glimmer in the dusk like glow-worms. As I gaze at it I dodge taxis and massive American cars, often painted in jagged black and white designs of teeth, or with undulating lines, battered and bashed as if they were ancient Greek sculptures. In the street around me I see girls, beautiful, each one seeming as if she had been made for some special and romantic tale of joy, heartbreak, or ecstasy.

The sheer feeling of the blazing power of Mexico is well shown in the Mariachis, those countless bands of musicians that have their accepted place in society. These little bands, consisting of from six to ten musicians, dress splendidly in a variety of fantastic uniforms, of which the most common is deep black velvet with silver facings, ruffled white shirts, huge black hats and high black boots.

No wedding is complete without its Mariachis, nor any outing. They are part of nearly every communal scene. I have seen them at remote bus staging points deep in the country, where, on the dusty road, they may wait outside a restaurant built from palm-branches, sitting in the shade in their gorgeous uniforms with their bright instruments on their knees until the bus emerges from the dusty road out of the jungle, and lurches to a halt. People climb down from it, some to buy Coca-cola, others to buy a song from the Mariachis.

The typical Mariachi group consists of one deep and vast-bellied guitar, two ordinary guitars, three violins, a couple of singers, two trumpets. Mainly the songs that the Mariachis sing are about 'amor' although some are about bull fights, football, or the agrarian revolution. The cost is about sixpence per player for each song. The Mariachis are known and loved and accepted by everyone. Even traditionally miserly characters have been known to pay out large quantities of money when the Mariachis make their appearance.

Other places where the Mariachis are always hanging about are on station platforms and around the bars. They have a sinister, conspiratorial air as they congregate in their vast cloaks and floppy hats.

If you are courting, one of the things to do with your girlfriend is to drive her in your car to the places where the Mariachis gather, to throw them a coin to play love songs, and embrace your girl-friend as the Mariachis cluster round serenading you. Some Mariachis also polish the windscreen and windows of the car, so you can see them correctly.

In Mexico City the best place for Mariachis is the Plaza Garibaldi, a sparse and squalid square without much vegetation. Here, up to fifteen different bands can be heard simultaneously; each vying with the next to produce a more exotic melody. The cross rhythms and counterpoint of this are quite amazing.

The music of the Mariachis is simple and beautiful. It is in the style of the waltz, and is said to date back to the brief period of French occupation, when Maximilian set up his gorgeous palace on the hill above Mexico City and tried to govern the Mexicans. He brought with him the waltz music of that time. And the Mexicans, recognising it as something that suited them, adopted it, and have retained it.

Coming from the obscure and teeming suburbs where they live, the Mariachis arrive at the Plaza Garibaldi in taxis and you can see their instruments stacked against the walls of the cafés and other buildings like weapons at a barracks.

Slowly I was learning more about the magic mushroom, both those varieties that grow in Mexico, and also others. My informant was an American.

'I was driving along a remote road and stopped to give a lift to two English girls who were waiting by the side of the highway. They seemed both friendly and intelligent and, when I dropped them off at their cottage, they mentioned knowing a botanist. They said that he had discovered what appeared to be a large mush-room by the side of a river about twenty miles outside of Johannes-burg. We got into discussion about what the mushroom was capable of doing. They mentioned that they might be able to obtain some of the mushrooms from our friend. I told them I would like to share it with them if that was possible. We arranged to meet the next day to pursue this further.

'I returned to their cottage the following afternoon and they showed me in their icebox, a large mushroom on a plate. The man had given them some information about it. He told them that the mushroom was commonly used by the Hottentots in some type of ritual. They would hunt in the forest till they came upon this species of mushroom, and then would clear a large circular area about it and allow it to grow to its maximum possible size. Then they would cut off the edges of the cap and eat them. The girls told me that they did not know what the effects produced by the mushroom would be like but they had been told that the experience was quite pleasant.

'The mushroom that lay at this point so tantalisingly in the icebox had a spherical cap about eight inches in diameter, was a greyish brown colour, and had two thick stalks underneath. I cut a small piece, less than half an ounce in weight, from the edge of the mushroom. I ate it. It had a very pleasant taste, not at all bitter. After this I retired to the garden.

'About twenty minutes passed without any noticeable reaction, except for an attack of hysterics, laughter without any reason. At this point a friend arrived to pick me up in his car. I had arranged, before I knew about this mushroom, to drive with him to Durban, a drive of some hundred and eighty miles.

'With some misgivings I joined him in the car. After we had been travelling for about half an hour I began to notice a feeling of being very light, a sense of weightlessness. It was a very happy feeling. And, as the journey continued, I began to experience a departure from what I would call normal reality.

'Slowly at first, and then more rapidly, I felt a mad rush in my mind, a sense of being riveted to the night sky outside the car. My vision became altered and there were auras around the stars and over the horizon. I felt as though I was sliding around on the car seat.

'I had no desire to speak and my friend, who was turning towards me from the wheel to say things, seemed to be just moving his lips. His words passed over, or rather through me.

'We finally arrived in Durban and stopped the car alongside a beach on the outskirts of the city. I walked out onto the sand and I felt an indescribable sensation – really contented, really good.

'It was as if I felt a tremendous sense of relief about something, but I couldn't really recall what the relief was from. I walked to a large rock on the beach and sat down on it. The tide was just coming in and there was a full moon over the ocean. I really felt at one with the elements around me. There was no sense of anxiety.

'The sea was now rushing in under the boulder I was on and I noticed how, as the waves came in, they seemed to shatter like glass against the rocks. The moon was in a completely clear sky and I felt as if hypnotised by it, as though the moon itself were drawing me into it. My head seemed to be filled with buzzing.

'There was a startling clarity about everything that I was thinking about. The sky and the moon seemed clearer than I had ever seen them before. Colours didn't change, but everything appeared brighter and clearer. Everything seemed to slip slightly sideways in time. Time seemed warped somehow. I felt definitely a part of the action occurring before me.

'At the height of the mushroom's effect, I had what I believe was a discourse with God. I just called God up and invoked Him, on an imaginary telephone, a sort of Dial-a-God system. I talked to this internal presence of Him about my problems, and I can remember receiving back simple straightforward answers to my complicated questions. It was as if a second person was inside me speaking to me about what was on my mind. I knew it was my own self somehow doing it, but it still astounded me and made some sort of sense, and seemed to me to be God.

'It must have been some time later that I began to realise that I had become drenched from the spray of the waves hitting the boulder. It was freezing cold but I didn't feel it at all, even though I was soaking wet.

'The air that I was breathing made me most exuberant. As I inhaled it I could feel it circulating in the back of my head and it also seemed to electrify my body. The moon began to look like the sun and its light was like sunlight, beating down on me with all the warmth of a midsummer day.

'I think the whole experience lasted for a total of eight hours. I was still sitting on the rock next morning when the sun came up. I felt exhausted from the night's experience and a bit jaded by all that had happened. I went further up the shore and I fell asleep and I can remember dreaming just one monosyllabic hum, endlessly endlessly humming, just running over and over in my brain, a sort of "dialling tone" to the way I was feeling, I thought.

'Before I ate the mushroom I was feeling unhappy. I thought

that I had problems, and these made me angry and bitter. Now I felt lovely.

'When I finally did fall asleep I had the feeling of somehow leaving my body completely. It was as if I was a few droplets of water falling into a large basin – all very peaceful and relaxing. Next day I was introverted. I wanted to make sense out of what had just happened but somehow I knew that that was impossible. I still felt abnormal. I was rather lethargic and very relaxed physically.

'I still regard the experience under the mushroom's influence as deeply religious.'

5

Into Indian Territory

The plane from Mexico City to Chiapas is flying low now, beneath us lies the dense jungle, amidst it just occasionally an angry river bearing forward its heavy depths of flood water.

We reach Tuxtla Gutierrez and I walk out of the little airport building and see my first palms and become happy. I eat in an open air restaurant, built round an arched central courtyard. Then I climb into the bus, and in it lurch slowly up into the sky, over mountains from which rise dense mists, and the way grows stranger and stranger, and on the road we pass Indian girls driving sheep across the empty countryside and there are loose horses cantering away from the bus across the hills, groups of barefoot Indian men looking astonished at the bus and dusky Indian women with little children on their backs.

Two or three hours later we arrive at San Cristobal de las Casas. This town has a Spanish Colonial central square, surrounded by arcades and with shrubs growing in its midst and concrete seats.

It is full of sad Indians. Women with little babies clasped to their backs, men, horny-footed, wearing their traditional Indian clothes, sitting round the arcades of the market, padding barefoot into the shops, peering about them with a wild look in their eyes. They pass the chemists' shops, they can't afford to buy anything there. Occasionally I see an Indian who has managed to get some money together heading back for his remote village, with rather ugly plastic cups and containers strapped to the basket on his back. And I wonder how many crops has he grown and bartered in exchange for these?

Many of the population of this province still go barefoot. Many can only speak Indian, no Spanish. And many are illiterate.

D. H. Lawrence, speaking of the Indian's relationship to nature, says, 'Nowhere more than in Mexico does human life become isolated, external to its surroundings and cut off from its environment. Even as you come across the plain to a big town and see the twin towers of the church peering around in the loneliness like two lost birds side by side, lifting their heads to look around in the wilderness, your heart gives a lurch, feeling the pathos, the isolated tininess of human effort.'

And writing of the Indians, he says: 'They spoke to each other in hardly audible crushed tones, as they always do, swerving away from us on the path, as if we were potential bold brigands. "Adios, adios, adios," say the women in suppressed voices, eyes lowered, swerving, neutral, past us on their self-contained sway-reared asses. . . . They laugh as if against their will, as if it hurt them, giving themselves away. . . .'

A piece of newspaper floating about the street says, 'Parties this fun-filled week . . . things perked up on the social scene this week with several fun fiestas and a cocktail-buffet at the Hotel Pierre in honour of the golf club project.

'Adele and Leonard Glenn had a cocktail party for more than fifty of their Mexican friends. The Glenns have just returned from the States and wanted to say a big hullo, calling all Gringos. A Mexican trio played all the Mexican numbers from W-a-a-a-a-y Back to Now.'

The hotel where I am staying interests me by its lack of any idea of what normally happens when one is staying in a hotel. This in turn makes me question my own idea of hotels and what should happen in them. Perhaps it is my attitude that is stuffy, rather than theirs that is unusual. Is it wrong of me to feel that it is strange that the two boys in whose hands the running of the hotel seems to be left enter my room at various times through the evening, hurl themselves down on the bed beside me, and engage me in lengthy conversation?

Is it wrong of me to think it so strange that, at intervals through the night, the window of my room is pushed open and a face peers in?

Is it wrong of me to think it strange to come back to my room and find the boys going through my luggage, that in the morning some of my clothes are missing and I am only able at last to retrieve them from the roof, where it is explained they have been taken so that they could be washed?

On the wall of my room is a notice. It says, 'Please conserve the reservoir of water and do not disperse the electrical energy.'

It isn't possible to lock the window or to open the door. And the attitude of the boys to me is one of strange, baleful, mournful suspicion and dislike, tempered with wild laughter. When I ask what the time is one of them asks, 'How much it cost?'

Later, a former Canadian small-plane pilot explains to me why these boys may be behaving like this. Probably, he says, they are lapsed Indians, Indian boys who have left their own tribe, and instead live a shadowy life in the city, aping the customs of the townspeople. Such Indian boys often become sad when they realise that for them there is no return to the Indian villages in the high plateaux, but similarly no future in the world they have entered. The boys in my hotel don't get wages, only their food and an occasional few pesos.

I hire a horse and a guide named Sergio and arrange for a trip into the Chamula Indian country. Mexican saddles have shoes instead of stirrups, vast stirrup leathers stamped and edged with devious and lovely designs, and the high pummel in front is used to tie the lassoo to when one is roping cattle.

We set off out of town, between the mean lines of one-storey houses, and soon we are climbing up an almost vertical hillside, the horses clambering up over rocks, and now, amidst the undergrowth, I can see Indians going their stealthy, secret, barefoot way, the men forging ahead with their machetes, wearing their traditional uniform of white straw hats and white blankets, followed at a discreet distance by their women, many of whom have babies tied to their backs with shawls. The babies peer out bright-eyed and happy at the world around them. Sometimes there are quite young girls and boys with them as well, aged perhaps three or four, loping along beside their mothers, having to run much of the way because their parents walk at such great speed. And the way they walk! Long since lost to us who don't cover long distances, and anyway wear shoes.

The local form of greeting is 'adios'. No one knows why. This has been translated by the children who have gone to school and learned a bit of English into 'goodbye', and so a stranger in these parts may be surprised to be greeted by those he meets along the way with a passionate 'goodbye'.

At one point we have to turn back because one of the bridges out of the town is considered not strong enough to allow us to pass. And now we are climbing up the precipitous slopes into the mountains. The horses are amazingly sure-footed as they pick their way up the almost perpendicular route which runs between the rocks. After we have climbed several hundred steep feet, sometimes on rocks and sometimes along a winding track running through the bright red soil, running between the vast trees of the encroaching jungle, we reach the brilliant yellow of a little lake, and there is an Indian sitting beside it, drinking water from his hat. Two women, with their long lanky hair falling down over their faces, sit beside him, their children strapped to their backs, and there are also two minute little girls of two or three sitting there.

We continue to climb, and Sergio informs me that we are coming near to Indian territory. A moment later and the path straightens out and becomes wider. Still this brilliant red flattened earth winds on between dense trees. To our left at one point the forest opens out and there is a little meadow of brilliant green shaven grass, sprinkled with buttercups. And now there are many more Indians gliding through the trees. They approach us, sometimes halt a moment as animals do when they see something that they don't at once recognise, then, rather than pass us, they turn abruptly left or right into the forest and continue their fast, creeping, sleuth-like progression, returning to the path when they are past us.

At one point Sergio seems bewildered and asks the way. The young Indian he asks says at first that he doesn't know which way the road goes. Then he points between the trees and says, 'That is the way.'

'Oh yes, I remember,' says my guide. 'Doesn't the other way lead to a village?'

'Yes,' says the Chamulan.

'What is the name of the village?' asks Sergio.

The Chamulan smiles, 'I do not know.'

Now the trees are rather taller, and have been hacked away here and there with blows from a machete. The green grass, sprinkled with little yellow and blue flowers, is filled with clear water, which wells up beside the horses' feet.

We pass a turning which is said to lead to some ruins, then we pass a man well-mounted on a horse with exotic harness spangled with silver studs, and not wearing Indian costume, but instead jeans and a denim jacket. He is accompanied by two men in Indian outfits of an extremely exotic style, exotic even for San Cristobal.

This man does reply when we ask him where he is going, but not naming anywhere that Sergio knows of. Sergio says, 'The Indians think nothing of walking or riding very long distances, even as much as two weeks seems to them to be not a particularly long journey, in order to go to market.

'Some of the wealthier Indians own fields in the valley. When the time comes to cut the wheat, they cut it and take it by lorry to the point nearest to the mountains. They unload it by the road, and live beside it and look after it. Others go back to the village to get help, and then hundreds of Indians come down from the mountain and carry the corn up to their homes in the mountains on their backs.'

We are riding along a fairly broad path of brilliant red earth, with the tall jungle trees arching up on either side. Every now and again to left and right it opens out into tiny uplands of brilliant green grass. On these are often little groups of Indians sitting, watching, totally silent, or standing in the wood so still, so silent, that you don't at once notice them.

Sergio says, 'These Indians seem always happy, always joyful, always laughing. When I first came here they laughed so much that I thought they must be laughing at me but that isn't so. They're just laughing because it is their nature.

'People get quite a wrong idea of them who only see them in the towns. When they arrive in the town, they are often on their guard. They're in enemy territory. They're afraid of the police too. The police never leave the town or go into the Indian lands. They just stand with their rifles at the ready outside the police station not daring to go very far. They know where their jurisdiction ends.

'But the Indians, once they get out of town and back into the jungle, become happy again. This is the place they know. There is a word in one of the Indian dialects which means "strolling through the jungle in a leisurely manner, hacking here and there with your machete". Theirs is a rich language. They have seventeen different words for the wind.

'The Indians here are extremely prosperous. The reason is that there is a lot of illegal alcohol brewing. They call it trago. These first villages we see are on the route to villages that are more remote. The packs on the back of those horses contain malt sugar for making the trago.

'The Indians feel uneasy in the towns and they're right. Since Spanish times they've been robbed and exploited by store-keepers. They can't count very fast. When you pay them they ask to be paid in one peso notes because they can't read the figures on paper money. Also, because they can't count and don't understand Spanish very well, they are a sitting target for the avaricious shopkeepers.

'Just as has happened in America, no respect is shown to these original settlers. Sometimes people go out from the towns and desecrate the crosses that the Indians erect on the outskirts of their villages, or on high places. But in their own villages they govern themselves.

'Some of the places where they live are called the "alcohol" country. They not only brew the stuff, but are drunk on it for much of the day. A few years back a German strayed into these remote villages. He didn't know the Indian language and he didn't come back. After a few days people went out to find him. They found him lying on the path to one of the villages, chopped up with a machete into many neat meat pieces.'

We pass an Indian farm, a hut made of adobe with mud brick walls and palm leaf roof, set in its little enclosure surrounded by maize, looking down over a long view of the village. In one of the fields is a very beautiful chestnut colt. A man stands beside one of the huts, shouting at us.

'What is he saying?' I ask.

'Oh, he's drunk.'

Another group of Indians hurries barefoot past us on their way to the market in the valley. All are heavily laden. One of the women has a vast bunch of white convolvuli on her head. Another is carrying by the legs fourteen chickens. Some carry baskets containing stuff that looks like coal, and others have nets full of the husks of corn on the cob. Some of the women also carry babies. The men have leather satchels and machetes, also stakes.

Chattering excitedly among themselves, a very large group of Indians pass by. Distributed among them are the vast frames of windows, various other bits of a house. One of them carries a large box with a loud speaker in it, and another has a car battery.

'Where are they bound for?' I ask.

'Who knows?' says Sergio. 'They must have some grandiose project far away in the mountains.'

The typical Indian house has a thatched roof and walls made of adobe bricks. I smile at one of the Indians and say to him, 'Adios.' 'Goodbye.' He says nothing. Often the Indians seem not to want to meet a stranger's eyes. I say again, 'Adios,' and smile at him. For a moment his eyes brush mine and he smiles back, life-lessly, painfully, as if it hurts him to smile. He hastily looks away.

Now the ground beside the path is strewn with the lovely blue shapes of gladioli. I ask the guide what is the significance of the occasional blazes on the trees. He says, 'Oh, there's no significance, that's just where the Indians hack them as they go by.'

And now at last we arrive in the Indian village. It consists of a little green grassy mound on which Indians are sitting or lying, a little hut with a Pepsi-cola sign on it, hung upside down. All around are the little Indian straw-hut houses, with their tidy fences and little crops of maize and children all over the place. In one yard an Indian woman is weaving a rug on an old-fashioned loom. No strait-jacket of tarmac or cobbles here to restrain the exuberance of grass and mud.

Large numbers of Indians are lying around on the grass, some-times they have stuck their stakes into the ground, stakes that point upwards like little flagstaffs amongst them. Various packages that they have with them, bound securely in leather, lie on the ground.

And now, to one side of the mound, I am invited into the school. This is a solidly built hut, made from adobe which has been white-washed outside, and inside is a long line of desks with about twenty little Indian children sitting there and a rather mangy looking teacher, also in the Chamula clothes. He invites me in, and I ask whether I may take a photograph. He says I can but as I raise the camera the children all dive underneath their desks as if I've cocked a gun.

It seems that the Indians believe that someone who takes a photograph of them thus has the reproduction of their image and can have power over them. Perhaps they're right.

A little plane goes soaring up into the sky. 'Whose plane is that?' I ask Sergio. 'Oh,' he says, 'one of those goddam fools that's trans-lating the Bible into Mayan.'

'Why are they doing that?'

Sergio enunciates drily, 'Why? Who knows? I said to the fellow, Surely you know that not one of the people you're translating

the Bible for, or very few, can even read? But they don't answer,
these fellows. They just go on flying around in their plane, waving
out of the windows.

'One of them's living in a caravan, he moved in by a great lake
near here; the Indians have a village in that part of the lake where
fish are most plentiful and the pastures are best.

'He planned to convert them to Christianity. But the Indians,
rather than face conversion, moved over to the other side of the
lake where fish were less plentiful and the land was far less good.

'These fellows could do some good. They could distribute
medicine, for instance, so that fewer Indian babies die in their first
months of life. They could hand out medicine and issue contraceptives. But actually, they do the reverse! They preach that con-
traception is evil. Breed. Breed, is their cry. The one single way
that they could help, they do harm instead. And they spend most
of their time in translating the Bible.'

The Indians seem very fine and strange as they cluster round
the arcades and porticos of the town. The principal ones are the
Chamulans, the Zinecantecans and the Tenehapa, and one can also
see other stranger Indians that come from far greater distances,
many days' trek through the forests.

The Chamulans wear ragged baggy knee-length trousers, and
hairy black or white serapes. The Zinecantecans wear light pink
striped blouses and very short shorts, and their multi-coloured
hat ribbons are worn tied up on the married men and dangling
loose on the bachelors. The Tenehapa wear knee-length black tunics
and flat straw hats. All except the men usually go barefoot.

I visit the house of a woman who has made herself champion of
the Indians. Her name is Trudi Blom. Trudi lives in a colonial
style house, rich in wood fires and with a succession of lovely patios.
The house is run by strapping girls educated in places like Long
Island. Trudi is a flamboyant figure who often changes her clothes
as many as three or four times in the day, and is always astound-
ingly and exquisitely dressed.

When her husband Franz was alive, there was a room in the
house where visiting Indians could always put up for the night.
This has now changed somewhat, and there is a fierce notice
outside saying, 'Es Una Casa Privada.' 'This is a private house.'

Some of the Indians keep themselves clean by means of a sweat bath. This is a little room too small to stand up in, with a fire at one end. One person comes in and strips naked and a second person, also naked, pours water onto the boiling stones round the fire. This produces an amount of steam, and in this primitive form of Turkish bath the Indians wash themselves.

Later we were shown into one of the Indian houses. Measuring about fifteen feet square, its walls were made of adobe and its roof of rushes. There was a fire burning in the centre of the earth floor, which the woman of the house kept scrupulously dusted. As we were standing talking, she remained at the side of the room, clutching her child to her, keeping her head away from us so that we couldn't see her face, giggling, shy.

My guide explained that up in the mountains people sleep on mats which they put down on the earth floor. Here, they were rich enough to afford rough plank beds. There were few other items visible in the place. I noticed an old oil lamp hanging from a beam, and a little shrine. Nothing much else. The cooking pots were kept outside under the thatched roof.

From various people in this town I was learning more about the Indians. A Canadian friend told me, 'I made some tape recordings of the rain song they have around here. Although they're nominally Christian, in fact the Indians make use of a large number of old-fashioned chants. There's quite a lot of Voodoo, and a lot of strange things go on in the mountains. Anyway, I recorded this chant that an old Indian woman was singing outside her hut one day, I didn't know what it was, but one of the Indians who was working for me said, "That's the rain chant, it brings rain".

'I went to another part of the country, and I wanted to do some other recordings, and in order to show them that the tape recorder was not harmful, I decided to play them something that I had already recorded. And it so happened that it was this same rain chant.

'One year later an Indian turned up on my doorstep. He had taken two weeks over the journey, and he had come to ask me to go back to his village to play them the rain chant again. "But," he said, "not quite so much this time. Last time it was very good, but it was too good. We had nothing but rain for two months!" '

Another story he told me concerned an attractive American girl who came down here to try to photograph the Indians. And, as usual, most of the Indians that she tried to photograph either ducked away or they threw stones at her.

At long last she came upon an Indian who seemed to be willing. The man was dressed in full ceremonial tribal gear. And he was most co-operative. He let her do whatever she wanted with him, posed this way and that, raised his arm, his leg, kneeled, looked this way and that, lay flat. She snapped away for half an hour, and, when she was finished, thanked him and gave him a peso. 'There's just one other thing, senora,' he said. She thought that he was going to ask her for more money. But no. Instead, from underneath his traditional tribal garments, he in turn produced a camera. He said, 'Now you must pose for me'. He was one of those Indians who has been given a scholarship to an American University. And he had her posing for a full hour, and he got her into some most interesting positions. 'And now, Ma'am,' says he, 'Hows about a date?'

The Indians are nominally Christians, but in fact they have basically taken over the churches the Spanish built for them and adapted them to their own rites. Sometimes, in these churches, Christ and the saints wear Indian garments. On at least one occasion, a local Indian saint was accused, while on a clandestine tour by night that included a visit to neighbouring villages, of having taken away some jewellery belonging to another saint. Since when he tours to this particular village no more.

Some of the saints are explosive. At festivals they are carried through the streets all day, and are then set on fire so that rockets concealed inside them explode violently into the night.

The Indians in these parts were never conquered. They fought successful battles with the Spaniards and remained free. Of other tribes it is said that they killed themselves to a man rather than submit to Spanish dominion. A whole tribe jumped over a cliff. But a greater adversary than any invading army now threatens the Indian way of life and culture. It's name is civilisation.

The Chamulans believe that each baby born has its double in an animal. The animal, bird, rabbit, or whatever, lives its wild life in the mountains, but if it should come to harm the human too will come to harm and it will be necessary to go out to the mountains to find the injured animal – and having found it, if possible cure it. Or it may have got caught in a snare, and you must set it free.

The Chamulans do not recognise some behaviour as being legal and other behaviour as being illegal. They will strongly condemn any acts that result in a person coming to harm, and 'the authorities', the law-givers of the Indians who wear distinctive clothes and are elected usually once a year, will punish such acts. But the idea of illegality apart from harm caused to an individual, is something that they don't recognise.

The women of the Chamulans have been described as 'shy, unkempt arrangements of dark shapeless folds of wool, hung with babies and bundles, dim backgrounds for the brilliant men, a covey of distant little peahens trotting behind the lustrous peacocks.' But I found the Chamula women beautiful.

As we were riding one day, my guide told me of the only other British that he'd ever met. This was a group of 'Sirs and Lords' who astounded everyone by their consideration for the horses, getting off and walking up the steepest places because they thought it was kinder. There was also an English lady 'of high rank' who put the Mexican cook to shame by the excellence of her cooking on the open flames. These same British carried with them small pills that they called Benzies, and what they called Instant Tequila, which was tequila concealed in the little tins which had contained the films for their cameras.

It turned out that I knew them well. One of them was indeed a close relative of mine.

One day an immensely venerable, tall, noble looking 'authority' approached me as I was speaking into my tape recorder in the precincts of a church. I think he must have thought that the tape recorder was a camera. The Indians hate cameras. Perhaps he was going to take action. I stood up, frantically shaking him by the hand, blurting out excuses that this was not a camera. Other Indians stood surlily around. I was alarmed. Angrily he spat out the words, 'One peso'.

An Indian gave me an account of marriage in his village. 'If a young man sees a girl that he likes, say, perhaps, by the water where she's gone to fill a cooking pot, he may go to his parents and say, "I saw her this afternoon, that's the girl I'd like for a wife". "Are you sure?" say his parents. "Yes, I'm sure". So then they will go together to the parents of the girl, and offer a present, which always includes alcohol, and the parents of the girl will probably not give a straight reply at once. They will say, "Why do you want *her*? She's a terrible girl, really a slut, she can't make tortilla, she's got a bad temper, you'd be mad to take her on."

'So the parents of the boy go away, and later they'll come back again, and so it will go on until the time that the parents finally say, yes, he can have her. He can have the girl, but he will have to work for six months in their fields until he's proved that he deserves her.'

The traditional way of life of all these Indians is threatened by the roads that are now being built through the forests to their villages. To begin with the Indians usually have objected to these roads, and occasionally tried to sabotage them. They also object to the schools that are built in their jungles. But later, they usually get a taste for such things.

Pointing to a distant tree just visible on the remote horizon, an American who has settled in this town said, 'Three of my staff live just under that tree. They walk the two hour walk here from there in the mornings and take the same walk back at night, clutching leftovers from my table, such as odd bits of cake, bones that people didn't eat, and unfinished stuff off the plates. They think nothing of it. And who can say whether their life is less rewarding than that of the commuter who drives his ninety minutes each way on the freeway every day in order to get home to his wife and family.'

The strangest of the surviving Indian tribes must be the Lacandrons. It is thought that these people, who live in the remotest jungle, the great forests of Eastern Chiapas, near the borders of Guatemala, are the direct descendants of the Mayans who were so advanced in mathematics, astronomy and the arts, before the Spanish came, over a thousand years ago.

Some strange catastrophe overtook them. To this day no one knows what stupendous cataclysm forced the Mayans to abandon the magnificent and extraordinary cities they built, and flee into the jungle. The Lacandrons live seven days' journey from the nearest roadhead. They have many gods, and every god has his wife. They believe that there is a heaven and a hell, and they call the stars God's seeds. The Lacandrons believe that the end of the world is imminent and that only through their prayers can they prevent it. Their land abounds in tropical fruit, fowl, wild animals, and flowers. They're polygamous. They bury their dead not far from their own homes, and build a little house over the grave.

They have never been Christianised, and still worship the sun and the moon, the water and the rains and corn, the mountains and the caves. They don't allow their menfolk to cut their hair. For hunting they use bows and arrows. In their fields they grow corn, beans, yucca, sweet potatoes, pineapples, sugar cane and other crops. In the forest they search for fruits and wild cacao and they hunt deer and wild boar.

The number of Lancandrons is diminishing, and there are now less than one hundred and fifty of them. Living in these last lost areas of the jungle, they are pitifully prone to catch diseases brought into the area by 'civilised' man, against which they have no built-in innoculation. The women wear the feathers of brightly coloured birds in their hair, made up of brilliant blues and canary yellows. They like to play on the flute, and accompany themselves by rattling gourds. They sleep in hammocks. There are so few of them that they are becoming inbred. And there is a real danger that the once mighty Mayans may disappear for ever.

Other disasters also threaten them. One family, wives and children of a man called Bor, were living on the banks of a river, and were accustomed to occasional visits from hunters who went canoeing on this river. One day a group of alligator hunters, coming down river in their canoes, stopped for the usual meal, and then suddenly seized all Bor's machetes, tools, and other belongings. The younger of the two wives fled and hid nearby in the jungle, but the older wife and the three small children were forced into the canoe and carried off against their will.

The smallest of these children, only a baby, made the alligator hunters so angry at her crying that they shot her and threw her body into the river for the alligators to eat. The hunters continued with the wife and other two children, and Bor never saw them again.

Bor, overwhelmed by this tragedy, could not bear to stay in the old place any more. He travelled many days with his younger wife Na Bor and her two boys through the jungle till he reached its edge. But Na Bor was pregnant and the journey exhausted her. She gave birth to a child and then disease overtook both her and the child and they died.

This accumulation of disaster proved more than Bor could take. He finally turned up in San Cristobal de las Casas with his one remaining child. I have seen this child – a quiet and delightful boy, eager to please.

It was necessary for Bor to find another wife, and he went about this by sitting in the market-place with some beads, swinging them around vociferously. This is the customary way of setting about getting a girlfriend in force among the Lacandrons. Unfortunately the Indian women of San Cristobal de las Casas were not familiar with this method of courtship, and viewed the bead-swinging Bor only with alarm and terror.

A man engaged in teaching the Indians better methods of agriculture told me, 'In medicine, Indians still believe in witchcraft. If they fall sick they practise all sorts of strange rites, and only at the last minute, perhaps too late, do they call a doctor. In agriculture they grow beans and wheat, *not* the best things for Indians to grow. In the last two years we have given the Indians many thousands of fruit trees. We have built roads. There was immense opposition to the road that we wanted to build through to the town of Chamula. But now that it has gone through there everyone is glad.'

As soon as a new road reaches an Indian town, the medicine wagon goes in too with loud-speaker on its top, selling quack medicine. A missionary told me, 'I remember at one fiesta, in a place where a road had just been built, the market place was crammed with men, and many of them were armed. Towards the end of the fiesta some *granaderos* arrived in a Land-Rover. In a moment about a hundred men had leapt on to ponies covered in sheep skins, guns, and exotic ornaments, fired their guns into the sky, and vanished rapidly up into the mountains, in a cloud of dust.'

We are climbing steeply up the rough red earth canyons and gullies. On our way lie great rocks planted in the earth. The paths reach up, undulating, rocky, precipitous. Beside them there are ferns and small purple flowers and butterflies erupt into the air as if cast out from a clenched hand. It is a beautiful morning. Dew is glistening on everything. Strange rocks emerge from the undergrowth. From their lichen-covered sides water drips and at the top of this steep ascent, five hundred or so feet up where the horses' hooves sink deep in the mud, there is, so they say, a place to which the Indians still come to put candles in front of a tree where there used to be a holy cross, now torn down by their enemies.

Smoke is rising from amongst the trees and there comes the musical thump of a machete, like a stroke on a timpano, from some obscure part of the forest. We ride farther, and reach an ancient signalling point from which the entire valley can be seen, stretched out below us, and the neighbouring peaks and other signalling points of other Indian villages.

Higher up still they say there was a cross, but it has been removed by those who hate the Indians. From this rocky shelf the Indians used to signal by means of 'orchestras, horns, or smoke'.

My guide says, 'Once this whole valley was a lake. The Indians stayed up here and signalled to each other across the water, from peak to peak.'

Further on we pass a pool of water – the only water available for some distance through these hills, a splash of yellow, and an Indian sitting by it, drinking from his hat. We reach a little village and stop to have a rest.

We haven't been sitting here long when a venerable man approaches us, raises his white and yellow hat, and after shaking our guide's hand explains that there is no right of way through here, and that we are not authorised visitors and that we are in danger because the people may think that we are inspectors come to investigate for signs of illegal brewing of trago (malt alcohol). There is a danger of shooting, he says. His teeth are bared in a smile.

With a compromise between dignity and speed we climb back on our horses and continue. Behind us the sound of guns fired into the sky. After many hours ride we come through a clearing to another Indian village, an idyllic looking place of orderly thatched huts, with a vast muddy market-place and a church at one end of it. The tops of the hills all round here are crowned with macabre crosses.

Whole families are sitting on the ground. One man, sitting on a small chair, is playing an accordion. There are bowls of pulque for sale, bundles of onions and slices of pineapple, beneath the tattered wooden shapes of stalls which have not had their roofs of skins put on yet.

My guide says, 'The red that the Indians wear at their festivals is the red of blood although they may not know it. Blood was thought to be the most valuable thing that could be offered to their god. But it is linked with the red of earth too. This is why they paint their houses and their sacrificial altars bright red.'

We are out in a beautiful valley of shaven lawn-grass growing from the red earth. We pass a ruined Spanish church where the little wooden crosses of the Indians stand on the open shaven hill-side and there is a lake of clear water, and black and white sheep and goats everywhere. It seems indeed the valley of Shangri-La, with the little pointed-topped huts stretching away among the fields of maize like somebody's dream of Utopia. Two horses lurch by in the water-filled meadows, their front feet tied together and their necks tied together with ropes. After many hours ride, we reach our objective. From the hills we see it first – a little white Spanish style church, decrepit.

There are no pews in the church. The floor is strewn with pine-needles. Wide plastic shrouds stretch across the roof. Little families are grouped together on the floor, drinking white alcohol from Coca-cola bottles and keeping up a persistent wailing sound. In front of them they put innumerable candles and are burning incense in little pots. The saints stand in rows along the side of the church, the old-fashioned ones near the back and the pristine and brightly painted ones near the front. Some have plastic rain-coats, gaudy handbags. A vast cross, apparently wound about with white paper, leans against the wall. Some of the Indians are very drunk.

Family after family are here, squashed up close together, fathers squashed against mothers, mothers squashed against children. They have drunk a lot and all the time they keep up a strange high-pitched wailing sound, a sort of hooting. They are praying. But in what language? And to whom?

6

Miss Wigley

'Serve yourself with another drink, I never serve, I am only served.'

I am in the apartment of one of Mexico's beautiful dusky burlesque dancers, by name, Ofelia. The gramophone is blaring away and the girl constantly dances, swaying as she talks, putting a silly expression on her face, talking, laughing, shaking her limbs about.

Her fifteen-year-old son is here, a boy who seems a little lost. Also in the apartment is a girl who works in a Mexican Record Company, and a Lesbian with close cropped hair, that I dislike instinctively – but it seems wrong to discriminate in this way.

'I am a Yucateca! Genuine Mayan!' the Lesbian cries in a low but raucous voice, strutting about like a turkey cock. She claps her hands and begins to nod excitedly to the music.

Ofelia says, 'When I was in England, I stayed with an English Lord and people say I broke up his marriage because I used to make him go out every night, every night dancing. And on Sundays we went to all the church services there were, one day Greek Orthodox, next Russian, next Catholicas.

'I used to lie in bed with him and we had his wife come up and serve us. People say I broke up his marriage. But that's very unfair.'

Once more she gallops away to continue her excited lyrical dancing. 'Olé,' cries the Lesbian, standing beside her, looking up into her eyes, raising her eyebrows up and down rapidly.

The bell rings and a middle-aged balding man enters. He wears spectacles with thick lenses and carries two bottles of whisky. Ofelia, crying with delight, makes him welcome by undulating in front of him. The Lesbian abruptly leaves.

A sad looking man enters and begins to tidy up the empty glasses.

'Are you concerned with the arts?' I ask the man with the whisky.

'But no. I run a factory that makes plastic shoes.'

The man grunts a little as he watches.

'What is this I hear about you, smashing a bottle of whisky at a party?'

'Oh,' says Ofelia, 'it was nothing. I had a friend and he bought me this present. I said, What, is that all you can do for a present for me? A bottle of whisky? That doesn't please me! And then I broke it. It was nothing.'

As he sits heavily beside her looking her up and down, the plastic shoemaker is still groaning to himself, his groans are audible over the raucous music. Ofelia continues to dance, completely enrapt in the joy of her totally self-centred life-giving personality. Talking to me so that the plastic shoemaker can't hear, she says, 'I have so many boyfriends. Men coming for me all the time.'

At dusk I stand at the top of the Latino-Americano building, Mexico's highest skyscraper, watching the ruddy evening clouds sweep in over the summits of the volcanoes. Then night falls, and the bar in which I stand is lit up occasionally by the searchlights of a passing jet.

And as I watch, I think of the wildness, the exoticism, the incredible grandeur of this country. The national drink here is tequila. They serve tequila in a tiny glass with a dish of salt and sliver of lime. You take a sip of tequila, followed by a lick of salt. The correct place to hold the salt is in the crook between the thumb and the first finger.

They have another drink called pulque, made from cactus. It is a white liquid the texture of thick milk with a strange, green, raw taste. It slays you. You buy it in a series of pulquerias. Its effects are more devastating than the German-style beer that is slowly replacing it.

I remember in one pulqueria a sad unshaven-faced Mexican, still wearing his hat, pointing out to me an old-fashioned French fashion magazine, showing fashions in vogue in France in about 1950, pointing out the breasts and buttocks of the girl with a lascivious look in his eyes, nodding at me sadly, repeatedly, fixing me with his wet watery red eyes. In a pulqueria little children will often turn up brandishing bottles which they want filled for their parents.

I remember a train journey, with crowds of people at the stations jostling against the train holding up bottles of pulque in their hands which they wanted to sell, holding them up like white candles.

Tequila is drunk often with Sangrita, a red hot drink like tomato ketchup. You drink alternately a sip of tequila and a sip of Sangrita, and this can be exciting, the alternation of hot taste and cold taste, it is all too easy to get into a perpetual motion so that you can't stop, the alternation of hot and cold is too fascinating.

I go to a show of the sort Ofelia dances at, and prominent among the performers is a girl advertised as 'Miss Wigley'. Here, in front of a vast audience, after a series of fairly unimportant acts, comes what we have been waiting for. A sort of primitive rite to the pleasures of sex, which begins with a procession of plump and desirable girls wearing fluffy blue bikinis, girls rather plumper and softer than one would find in a European show, entering in a long line, carrying above their heads large paniers of white flowers.

They are followed by a group of men whose trousers have a large blue flower painted over the crotch. Then Miss Wigley herself enters and begins to dance. A rather raffish man at the back is striking a drum in an imperative rhythm. As Miss Wigley dances he bangs on his drum which is amplified to a tremendous hissing volume, and he shouts out 'Dale! Dale!' His eyes are fixed on her, and much of the time the girl has her back to the audience, one leg is raised and she shakes herself around the one leg that remains on the floor as the man shouts, 'Dale! Dale!' At intervals during Miss Wigley's passionate dance the other girls come on, a lovely chorus, chanting, carrying their platters laden with white flowers. Then they disappear again.

Miss Wigley's dance reaches a climax, and she collapses on the floor. But the drumming doesn't stop. It continues quietly to patter and Miss Wigley begins to revive again, and then the drummer suddenly mentions quietly, hopefully, 'Dale de nuevo!' And he thumps his hands on the drum once more, and Miss Wigley begins once more to dance.

Now there comes a dramatic sketch in which a man, in a hotel, listens through the wall to a girl whose boyfriend is trying to get some shoes that he's bought her onto her feet. The girl comments, 'It's too small, I can't possibly get it in, but I want to, my mother is so anxious that I should.' And other such simple jokes. Then comes more stripping.

One of the later acts I enjoy most is an Indian husband, in full tails, who, to the sound of crashing cymbals, slowly undresses his prim upright-standing bride, a girl clothed entirely in veils that are a whiter shade of pale. With each fresh garment he pulls off, as he uncovers ankle, belly, or finger, there is a massive crash of drums from behind the scenes, and the tail-coated figure appears totally smitten with the beauty of the girl, which has the curious effect of hurling him violently backwards across the floor, where, in a crouching position, he revolves rapidly, semi-horizontal.

Sometimes he picks the girl up and tosses her around above his head in rapid circles, perhaps as a sign of his appreciation. Finally, as he uncovers her breasts, he ricochets backwards even further than before, reacting as if he's been blinded, or as if a heavy rock has hit him. Recoiling, withdrawing from those small breasts that point at him like a pair of angry machine guns, he once more violently rotates on the floor, before staggering to his feet and carrying her round sky-high on his shoulders.

A girl wearing a bikini painted with jungle-like devices, and brandishing a whip, enters holding both her arms above her head which bears a proliferous mass of black hair. She waves her whip in the air and lo and behold, there lopes into sight a great black monkey. The monkey is naughty, makes gestures that the girl dislikes, so she whips him. She launches into an elaborate and fairly beautiful dance routine, but the monkey spoils this by throwing cart wheels and picking at fleas beneath his armpits or beating his chest, as the lovely girl cartwheels and cavorts about him.

Then all is changed. To the enthusiastic shouts of the audience the monkey begins to undress the girl. He hurls her down on the floor. She lies, her back to the audience. First, all the audience can see is her expanse of dark hair, and her breasts sticking up peremptorily like Popocatepetl and Ixtacihuatl, those two choice volcanoes. But suddenly she is on her feet again and wrestling with the monkey. She whips the poor animal as hard as she can round his furry haunches. But he is winning. He forces his evil desires on the girl. That's when she produces from her belt a sword, and with remarkable dexterity she thrusts it into him, and the monkey falls on the ground just an inanimate heap of fur.

The Mexicans don't seem to applaud a lot. Only when they see something that takes their fancy. There was a girl that they seemed to like more than any of the others, and their applause was an ovation, ecstatic, as she pranced about, revealed, then hid once again, then revealed her pointed breasts.

7

The Hotel Blitz

My apartment in the Hotel Blitz is one of the most curious I have been in. When I first opened the door I found myself in a small room with many windows, all of which had been painted on the inside with thick yellow paint. Thus no light was able to penetrate through them.

I thought it strange that these windows had been thus painted, and going to one, flung it open. No rush of daylight into the room followed this expansive gesture. Through the broad window was visible only a narrow and fetid chimney. I crossed the room and flung open the other window. But once again the effect was not as I had hoped. This window gave onto a thin courtyard, very dim, surrounded by the similar windows of other rooms, rising up to a very great height and roofed at the top with transparent corrugated plastic. This room was so curious, and the price asked for it so outrageous, that I decided to stay here.

Outside, where work goes on day and night on the Underground, the way is lit by tins filled with paraffin which flare slowly through the night. A lorry has just knocked over one of these tins, and one of its tyres is on fire. The driver, trying to put it out, is driving faster and faster along the road. The flames grow wilder as he disappears from sight round a corner, a lorry balanced on a ball of fire.

Tiring of the blank-windowed room and its deep gloom, I move to another place, not a hotel but a boarding house. It is a Spanish Colonial edifice, with one huge stained-glass window, covered outside by a curtain which is moved across during the day to keep the sun out. The entrance hall has a main staircase which climbs up towards the roof of this vaulted chamber and then turns across it along a narrow bridge.

The boarding house is run by a woman called Señorita Mundoz and her brother. Her brother is a sad man, who paces up and down for much of the day along a spacious neo-Gothic chamber, wringing his hands. As for her, she had a tumour on the brain two years ago and can remember nothing before that – her allegedly aristocratic upbringing, the hacienda in the country – all this wiped out.

Has Britain made any mark on this country whatever? Is there anything to remind one of home? One day, wandering through a slum area of Mexico City amid the brightly painted one-storey little houses and courtyards whose every room seems to house a numerous family, I see a large notice on the outside of a building somewhat taller and more windowless than the others, *Ejército de Salvación* – Salvation Army.

Hurrah! Here is visual evidence of at least one British export to reach Mexico's fair shore! There are ten or twelve boys, bare to the waist, kicking an old tin can around in the street. I watch them as I bang on the heavy iron doors that clangingly reverberate as I hit them.

A wait amidst the intense heat of the Mexican August afternoon – that sort of afternoon which is so hot that the houses themselves seem overwhelmed with the heat, part visible because they are so bright, seemingly flattened into the ground by the sun. It is the sort of afternoon when groups of mangy dogs in fours and fives set out to hunt through the hot streets, and someone accustomed to wider spaces can have a feeling of claustrophobia.

I bang again. No one comes to the door. Eventually the door is opened by a small man who leads me into a long, hot, empty courtyard, with doors along one side, a faded notice saying '*Sangre y Fuego*', and a hole in the midst of its concrete enabling one to see down into a rather putrid drain. There comes a shout from a raised terrace at the end of the patio. The man who let me in says to me in an awed voice: 'El capitán!'

So! The Salvation Army keeps its military rank here as well. El capitán, in his shirt sleeves, appears for a moment at the balcony above. Although it's two in the afternoon he is shaving. Thinking I am a down-and-out looking for a lodging for the night, he shouts somewhat harshly for me to wait a minute. I stand in a patch of shade and the small man comes and engages me in conversation.

'There are many bad men around here, many ladrones, thieves,' he mentions. Various other inhabitants of the hostel come and join us and stand around, peering at me. With considerable dignity at length the captain appears, a well-built man wearing a shirt and grey trousers.

Once he has established that I am not after a bed for the night and has satisfied himself as to my solvency by various searching questions (such as did I come in a train or a boat, how much did it cost, and how long did it take) his manner changes, and in a moment he is offering to take me for a drive in his car to show me the famous castle of Chapultepec, the Reforma, and the other sights of town. I explain that my reason for being here is to learn something of the life of the poor as well as the rich. This answer appears to please the man even more.

'Well, first, I expect you'd like to see round the hostel,' he says. He explains that he has three dormitories, each capable of accommodating thirty men. There is Number One dormitory for the saved, from which, he explained, men are expected to go out and find jobs for themselves. Number Two dormitory, for those who are half saved. Finally he pulls open the doors of the dormitory which stands closest to the street, and whose barred windows look out on the street. 'And here is Number Three dormitory. This is where we put the men that we take off the streets. It is called the Dormitory of the Fallen.'

I get the feeling that very few beds in any of these dormitories are occupied at the moment. But I may be wrong about this. In all I only see about five or six men in the hostel.

'Now I must show you the temple,' says the Captain. He leads me back out into the street, and we walk beneath the hot sun, till we reach another tin door, painted dark red like the first. He bangs heavily on this and an old lady opens it for us. We go in, towards an open space with low corrugated iron covered buildings baking all around it and a concrete centre like a parade ground. I am struck by a certain quality, or rather lack of quality, in these mean buildings. Unlike the Catholic Church, the Salvation Army has never concerned itself with that architectural peace and placidity that other religions have aspired to in their attempts to help the poor. Compared to Catholic churches that I have seen, the place seems mean – yet practical. As we enter the parade ground another voice hails us from above. This is another captain, who, peering down, asks severely what we are up to. I explain, and, like the other man, he smiles in relief that I am not another down-and-out and invites me upstairs for a coffee.

'I have been in London and I am sorry I cannot give you a cup of tea,' he says with a smile.

'Where did you live when you were in London?' I ask.

'Next to the Queen!'

'Next to the Queen?'

'The Ejército de Salvación at the Hostel close to the Queen!'

He explains, as we look through the window at the empty parched parade ground, that this is the training college for new ministers in the Mexican Salvation Army. 'We have two classrooms, a chapel, a dining-room, and they sleep in dormitories.'

Again I am struck by the fact that there don't seem to be any people around.

'Where are the student ministers?' I ask. 'There don't seem to be any here. Are they away on holiday?'

He laughs politely at this, and explains, 'The officers of the Ejército de Salvación do not have holidays. They are out doing field work, helping the poor!'

I go to a service in the green-painted room that serves as a chapel. A little girl is booming away at a vast drum with *Sangre y Fuego* written on it and there are children singing to Mexican words those catches which the Salvation Army has made famous throughout the world. People are clapping their hands and swaying in time to the music. Now a new sound can be heard mixing with the boom of the drum. It is the afternoon torrential rain which falls regular as clockwork in Mexico at this time of day. The noise is deafening, and the few late worshippers arrive soaked to the skin. Occasionally mothers come to the tin door of the chapel and call loudly for their children. A third captain, his eyes flashing, glancing down with considerable authority preaches an impetuous sermon, full of blood and fire. The service is open-ended, unlike the services familiar to those who are brought up in the Church of England or similar more orthodox organisations, and people come and go throughout.

Later, the captain says to me, quietly, 'What do you think of the British youth, what is the reason for this terrible problem?'

'What problem are you referring to?'

'Well, you know, all these hippies, the flower people, the students, the extraordinary fashions in which Britain leads the world. Why can it be? For instance, in London I was at the Major Lords procession. It was very beautiful, you know, with the moustaches and the dignity and ceremonial, yes, but what were people looking at? Not at that, not at the ceremonial, but at the young girl walking in front, who had got a mini-skirt right up to *here*.'

'That's not a mini-skirt, that's an apron,' comments the second captain.

'Yes, you are right. And no one was looking at the Major Lord, they were all looking at the girl, one man had binoculars and he was trying to see her sex. I borrowed the binoculars too. And d'you know, when I looked through them, I saw her sex too. And that her thighs were all covered with bugs and flies.

'I had a feeling that she was trying to make a mockery of the procession.'

'Yes, and did you hear about what happened at the Airport?' asks the second captain. 'Well, there was a German girl, she was wearing a see-through blouse, and then as she waited to go through the customs, she took off all her clothes except her bra and pants, and then she took her brassiere off as well! She stayed there till the police came and asked her to put on her clothes again. Some of the women left the queue but the men stayed. She said she was hot. What has got into you Europeans?'

It was in Mexico City that I met Variety. Sultry, gazing out at the world from dark eyes beneath long dark hanging hair, she wore on her white shoulders a constellation of black birth marks as if she had been covered with a robe of negative stars.

Frequently this strangely named girl who had in fact been born in Uruguay would smoke hashish from what she called 'an absurd machine' – this was a shallow pie dish over which she had stretched silver paper.

At one side of the silver paper was a hole about the size of the end of a pencil through which one inhaled. Inside the dish there was ice. At the other end, a number of little holes over which the hash, lit lightly with a match, was spread. Variety spent many hours each day inhaling from her 'absurd machine'.

'I have a friend who could help you find your way to the magic mushrooms without leaving Mexico City,' she said one day. 'I didn't want to tell you till now, but now I know you well enough.

Indians and Mestizzos

A Mariachi getting out
his violin

More primitive music

He uses books that have no insides to transport the distilled ashes of the mushrooms round the world.

'He is a big man, big. He has contacts with another who runs a yacht and another with an aeroplane. They're all big people, oh, big!'

'Great!' I said. 'When can you arrange for me and him to meet?'

'It is not necessary for you to meet. I can get it all. How many of the mushrooms would you like?'

'I suppose – a dozen.'

'One dozen? Is that all?'

Variety's face fell.

'It would have been easier to order one or two *hundred*.'

'All right, never mind.'

'I will see what I can do.'

I didn't see Variety for a few days after that. I saw her next at the private view of a popular art gallery. She immediately placed her hand over her mouth as if in a small yawn.

'Ask me nothing about that absurd thing,' she urged me in a hoarse whisper. 'At the frontier, did you hear?'

'Er. . . . ?'

'Not for the mushrooms for they are not evil. No, for other things. . . . Yes I am sorry to say. . . . Too bad. . . .'

The girl stretched her arms above her head and her body was for a moment pleasantly outlined against a background of woods and boscages in the paintings that we'd been summoned to see.

'It's all right,' I said, 'I'm used to it.

'I know that the meeting between me and the magic mushrooms, not to speak of the eating by me of the magic mushroom – is not a thing that can be hoped will happen easily.'

'Too bad,' sighed Variety. 'Now come and "have a go" with my absurd machine.'

c

8

Divine Mushrooms

'I do not recall which of us, my wife or I, first dared to put into words back in the forties, the surmise that our remote ancestors perhaps 4,000 years ago, worshipped a divine mushroom.'

These words were used by R. Gordon Wasson to the Mycological Society of America, at Stillwater, Oklahoma, in 1960.

'If we are right,' he continued, 'and little by little the accumulating evidence seems to be in our favour – then this Middle American cult of a divine mushroom, this cult of "God's flesh" as the Indians in pre-Columbian times called it, can be traced back to about 1500.' He continued, 'I shall take you now to the monolingual villages in the uplands of Southern Mexico. Only a handful of the inhabitants have learned Spanish. The men are appallingly given to the use of alcohol, but in their minds the mushrooms are utterly different, not in degree, but in kind. Of alcohol they speak with the same jocular vulgarity that we do. But about the mushrooms they prefer not to speak at all, at least when they are in company and especially when strangers, white strangers, are present. If you are wise, you will talk about something, anything else. Then, when evening and darkness come and you are alone with a wise old man or woman whose confidence you have won, by the light of a candle held in a hand and talking in a whisper, you may bring up the subject. Now you will learn how the mushrooms are gathered, perhaps before sunrise, when the mountainside is caressed by the pre-dawn breeze, at the time of the new moon, in certain regions only by a virgin. The mushrooms are wrapped in a leaf, perhaps a banana leaf, sheltered thus from irreverent eyes, and in some villages they are taken first to the church, where they remain for some time on the altar, in a jicara or gourd bowl. They are never exposed to the market place but passed from hand to hand by pre-arrangement. I could

66

talk to you a long time about the words used to designate these sacred mushrooms in the languages of the various people who know them. The Aztecs before the Spaniards arrived called them *teo-nanacatl,* God's flesh. And I need hardly remind you of a disquieting parallel, the designation of the elements in our Eucharist : "Take, eat, this is My body. . . ." and again, "Grant us therefore Gracious Lord, so to eat the flesh of Thy dear Son. . . ." But there is one difference. The orthodox Christian must accept by faith the miracle of the conversion of the bread into God's flesh : that is what is meant by the doctrine of transubstantiation. By contrast, the mushroom of the Aztecs carries its own conviction; every communicant will testify to the miracle that he has experienced. . . .

'In 1953 our mulateer had travelled the mountain trails all his life and knew Spanish, though he could neither read nor write, nor even tell time by a clock's face. We asked him why the mushrooms were called "That which brings forth". His answer was breathtaking in its sincerity and feeling, was filled with the poetry of religion, and I quote it word for word as he gave it :

> *El honguillo viene por si mismo no se sabe de donde*
> *Como el viento que viene sin saber de donde ni porque.*

> The little mushroom comes of itself, no one knows whence.
> Like the wind it comes and we know not whence nor why.

'We know that today there are many curanderos who play on the cult, each according to his lights, some of them consummate artists, performing the ancient liturgy in remote huts before miniscule congregations. With the passing years they will die off, and as the country opens up, the cult is destined to disappear. They are hard to reach, these curanderos . . . after all, would you have it any different? What priest of the Catholic Church will perform Mass to satisfy an unbeliever's curiosity?'

Wasson went on to talk of the Eleusinian mysteries. 'From the writings of the Greeks and from a fresco in Pompeii,' he said, 'we know that the initiates of the mysteries of Eleusis drank a potion. And in the depths of the night they beheld a great vision and the next day were so awestruck that they felt they would never be the same as before.'

A writer called Aristides, in the second century A.D., says Wasson, 'pulled the curtain aside for an instant with this fragmentary description of the Eleusinian mystery, "Eleusis is a shrine common to the whole earth, and of all the divine things that exist among men, it is both the most awesome and the most luminous. In what place in the world have more miraculous tidings been sung, where have the dromena called forth greater emotion, where has there been greater rivalry between seeing and hearing?" '

Wasson comments, 'May it not be significant that the Greeks were wont to refer to mushrooms as "the food of the Gods", *bromatheon*, and that Porphyrius is quoted as having called them 'nurslings of the Gods', *theotrophos*?

'Thus it comes about that, thanks to the achievements of our biological chemists, we may be on the brink of rediscovering what was common knowledge among the ancient Greeks. I predict that the secret of the mysteries will be found in the indoles, whether derived from mushrooms or from higher plants, or, as in Mexico, from both. These indoles, psilocybin and psilocin tryptamine are derivatives of the indole family of substances, and these are the active agents in some of the Mexican mushrooms.

'I would not be understood as contending that only these substances (wherever found in nature) bring about visions and ecstasies. Clearly some poets and prophets and many mystics and ascetics seem to have enjoyed ecstatic visions that answer the requirements of the ancient mysteries and that duplicate the mushroom agapé of Mexico. I do not suggest that St John of Patmos ate mushrooms in order to write the Book of the Revelations. Yet the succession of images in his vision, so clearly seen and yet such a phantasmagoria, means for me that he was in the same state as one bemushroomed. Nor do I suggest for a moment that William Blake knew the mushroom when he wrote his telling account of the clarity of "vision". The prophets describe what they saw in a vision as real and existing men, whom they saw with their imaginative and immortal organs; the Apostles the same; the clearer the organ the more distinct the object. A spirit and a vision are not, as the modern philosophy supposes, a cloudy vapour or a nothing; they are organised and minutely articulated beyond all that mortal and perishing nature can produce. He who does not imagine in stronger and better lineaments and in better and stronger light than his perishing eye can see, does not imagine at all.

'This must sound cryptic,' says Wasson, 'to one who does not share Blake's vision or who has not taken the mushroom. The advantage of the mushroom is that it puts many (if not everyone) within reach of this state without having to suffer the mortifications of Blake and St John. It permits you to see, more clearly than our perishing mortal eye can see, vistas beyond the horizons of this life, to travel backwards and forwards within time, to enter other planes of existence, even (as the Indians say) to know God. It is hardly surprising that your emotions are profoundly affected, and you feel that an indissoluble bond unites you with the others who have shared with you in the sacred agapé. All that you see . . . has a pristine quality, the landscape, the edifices, the carvings, the animals – they look as though they had come straight from the maker's workshop. This newness of everything – it is as though the world had just dawned – overwhelms you and melts you with its beauty. Not unnaturally, what is happening to you seems to you to be freighted with significance, beside which the humdrum events of every day are trivial. All these things you see with an immediacy of vision, that leads you to say to yourself, "I am seeing for the first time, seeing direct, without the intervention of mortal eyes". (Plato tells us that beyond this ephemeral and imperfect existence here below, there is another ideal world of archetypes, where the original, the true, the beautiful pattern of things exists for evermore. Poets and philosophers have pondered and discussed his conception. It is clear to me where Plato found his ideas; it was clear to his contemporaries too. Plato had drunk of the potion in the temple of Eleusis and had spent the night seeing the great vision.)

'The bemushroomed person is poised in space, a disembodied eye, invisible, incorporeal, seeing but not seeing. In truth, he is the five senses disembodied, all of them keyed to the height of sensitivity and awareness, all of them blending into one another most strangely, until the person, utterly passive, becomes a pure recepter, infinitely delicate of sensation. . . . As your body lies there in its sleeping bag, your soul is free, loses all sense of time, alert as it never was before, living an eternity in a night, seeing infinity in a grain of sand. What you have seen and heard is cut as with a stylus within your memory, never to be effaced. At last you know what the ineffable is, and what ecstasy means. Ecstasy! The mind harks back to the origin of that word. For the Greek *ekstasis* meant the flight of the soul from the body. Can you find a better word than that to describe the mushroom state?

'In common parlance among the many who have not experienced ecstasy, ecstasy is found; and I am frequently asked why I do not reach for mushrooms every night. But ecstasy is not found. Your very soul is seized and shaken until it tingles. After all, who will choose to feel undiluted or to float through that door yonder into the divine presence?

'Perhaps with all our own modern knowledge we do not need the divine mushrooms any more. Or do we need them more than ever? Some are shocked that the key even to religion might be reduced to a mere drug. On the other hand, the drug is as mysterious as it ever was : "Like the wind it cometh we know not whence, nor why". Out of the mere drug comes the ineffable, comes ecstasy.

'If our classical scholars were given the opportunity to attend the rite of Eleusis, to talk with the priestess, what would they not exchange for that chance? They would approach the precincts, go into the hallowed chamber, with the reverence born of the texts venerated by scholars for aeons. How propitious would that frame of mind be, if they were invited to partake of the potion ! Well, those rites take place now, unbeknownst to classical scholars, in scattered dwellings, humble, thatched, without windows, far from the beaten track, high in the mountains of Mexico, in the stillness of the night, broken only by the distant barking of a dog or the braying of an ass.'

The use of the magic mushroom in one form of religion has been described in *The Teachings of Don Juan: A Yaqui Way of Knowledge* by Carlos Castaneda.

Don Juan, Carlos Castaneda's Indian teacher of religious mysteries, used three hallucinogenic plants : Peyote (*lophophore Williamsii*), Jimson weed (*Datura Inoxia Syn D. Meteloides*) and a mushroom, possibly *Psilocybe Mexicana*.

The importance of the plants for him was their capacity to produce stages of peculiar perception in a human being. One of the three hallucinatory mixtures consisted of leaves and flowers and mushrooms mixed together and smoked.

'The real secret of the mixture lies in the mushrooms,' Don Juan said. 'They are the most difficult ingredients to collect. The trip to the place where they grow is long and dangerous, and to select the right variety is even more perilous. There are other kinds of mushrooms growing alongside which are of no use; they would spoil the good ones if they were tried together. It takes time to know the mushrooms well in order not to make a mistake. Serious harm would result from using the wrong kind – harm to the man and to the pipe. I know of men who have dropped dead from using the foul smoke.

'As soon as the mushrooms are picked they are put inside a gourd, so there is no way to reject them. You see, they have to be torn to shreds in order to make them go through the narrow neck of the gourd.'

'How long do you keep the mushrooms inside the gourd?'

'For a year. All the other ingredients are also sealed for a year. Then equal parts of them are measured and ground separately into a very fine powder. The little mushrooms don't have to be ground because they become a very fine dust by themselves; all one needs to do is to mash the chunks. Four parts of mushrooms are added to one part of all the other ingredients together. Then they are all mixed and put into a bag like mine.'

Castaneda's initiation took place in the years 1961-65. This is how he describes first taking the mushrooms, which in this case were being smoked, 'The thought of refusing the pipe and running away crossed my mind for an instant; but Don Juan demanded again – still in a whisper – that I take the pipe and smoke. I looked at him. His eyes were fixed on me. But his stare was friendly, concerned. It was clear that I had made the choice a long time before; there was no alternative but to do what he said.

'I took the pipe and nearly dropped it. It was hot! I put it to my mouth with extreme care because I imagined its heat would be intolerable to my lips. But I felt no heat at all.

'Don Juan told me to inhale. The smoke flowed into my mouth, and seemed to circulate there. It was heavy! I felt as though I had a mouthful of dough. The simile occurred to me although I had never had a mouthful of dough. The smoke was also like menthol, and the inside of my mouth suddenly became cold. It was a refreshing sensation. "Again! Again!" I heard Don Juan whispering. I felt the smoke seep inside my body freely, almost without my control. I needed no more urging from Don Juan. Mechanically I kept inhaling.

'Suddenly Don Juan leaned over and took the pipe from my hands. He tapped the ashes gently on the dish with the charcoals, then he wet his finger with saliva and rotated it inside the bowl to clean its sides. He blew through the stem repeatedly. I saw him put the pipe back into its sheath. His actions held my interest.

'When he had finished cleaning the pipe and putting it away, he stared at me, and I realised for the first time that my whole body was numb, mentholated. My face felt heavy and my jaws hurt. I could not keep my mouth closed, but there was no saliva flow. My mouth was burning dry, and yet I was not thirsty. I began to sense an unusual heat all over my hand. A cold heat! My breath seemed to cut my nostrils and upper lip every time I inhaled. But it didn't burn; it hurt like a piece of ice.

'Don Juan sat next me, to my right, and without moving held the pipe sheath against the floor as though keeping it down by force. My hands were heavy. My arms sagged, pulling my shoulders down. My nose was running. I wiped it with the back of my hand, and my upper lip was rubbed off! I wiped my face, and all the flesh was rubbed off! I was melting! I felt as if my flesh was actually melting. I jumped to my feet and tried to grab hold of something – anything – with which to support myself. I was experiencing a terror I had never felt before. I held onto a pole that Don Juan keeps stuck on the floor in the centre of his room. I stood there for a moment, then I turned to look at him. He was still sitting motionless, holding his pipe, staring at me.

'My breath was painfully hot (or cold). It was choking me. I bent my head forward to rest it on the pole, but apparently I missed it, and my head kept on moving downward beyond the point where the pole was. I stopped when I was nearly down to the floor. I pulled myself up. The pole was there in front of my eyes! I tried again to rest my head on it. I tried to control myself and to be aware, and kept my eyes open as I leaned forward to touch the pole with my forehead. It was a few inches from my eyes, but as I put my head against it I had the queerest feeling that I was going right through it.

'In a desperate search for a rational explanation I concluded that my eyes were distorting depth, and that the pole must have been ten feet away, even though I saw it directly in front of my face. I then conceived a logical, rational way to check the position of the pole. I began moving sideways around it, one little step at a time. My argument was that in walking around the pole in that way, I couldn't possibly make a circle more than five feet in diameter;

if the pole was really ten feet away from me, or beyond my reach, a moment would come when I would have my back to it. I trusted that at that moment the pole would vanish, because in reality it would be behind me.

'I then proceeded to circle the pole, but it remained in front of my eyes as I went around it. In a fit of frustration I grabbed it with both hands, but my hands went through it. I was grabbing the air. I carefully calculated the distance between the pole and myself. I figured it must be three feet. That is, my eyes perceived it as three feet. I played for a moment with the perception of depth by moving my head from one side to the other, focusing each eye in turn on the pole and then on the background. According to my way of judging depth, the pole was unmistakably before me, possibly three feet away. Stretching out my arms to protect my head, I charged with all my strength. The sensation was the same – I went through the pole. This time I went all the way to the floor. I stood up again. And standing up was perhaps the most unusual of all the acts I performed that night. I thought myself up! In order to get up I did not use my muscles and skeletal frame in the way I am accustomed to doing, because I no longer had control over them. I knew it the instant I hit the ground. But my curiosity about the pole was so strong I "thought myself" up in a kind of reflex action. And before I fully realised I could not move, I was up.

'I called to Don Juan for help. At one moment I yelled frantically at the top of my voice, but Don Juan did not move. He kept on looking at me, sideways, as though he didn't want to turn his head to face me fully. I took a step towards him, but instead of moving forward I staggered backward and fell against the wall. I knew I had rammed against it with my back, yet it did not feel hard; I was completely suspended in a soft spongy substance – it was the wall. My arms were stretched out laterally, and slowly my whole body seemed to sink into the wall. I could only look forward into the room. Don Juan was still watching me, but he made no move to help me. I made a supreme effort to jerk my body out of the wall, but it only sank deeper and deeper. In the midst of indescribable terror, I felt that the spongy wall was closing in on my face. I tried to shut my eyes but they were fixed open.

'I don't remember what else happened. Suddenly Don Juan was in front of me, a short distance away. We were in the other room.

I saw his table and the dirt stove with the fire burning, and with the corner of my eye I distinguished the fence outside the house. I could see everything very clearly. Don Juan had brought the kerosene lantern and hung it from the beam in the middle of the room. I tried to look in a different direction, but my eyes were set to see only straight forward. I couldn't distinguish, or feel, any part of my body. My breathing was undetectable. But my thoughts were extremely lucid. I was clearly aware of whatever was taking place in front of me. Don Juan walked towards me, and my clarity of mind ended. Something seemed to stop inside me. There were no more thoughts.'

Further claims about the magic mushroom were made by Andrija Puharich, the founder and director of a parapsychological laboratory in Maine. As a doctor he had stimulated an interest in 'the neurochemical and psychochemical aspects of the human nervous system'. The main activity of his laboratory was the systematic testing of people believed to possess Extra Sensory Perception. These tests were held, so he claimed, under scientific conditions.

Puharich became interested in a sculptor called Harry Stone who went into a trance. This trance was apparently induced when he touched an Ancient Egyptian cartouche, and in this first trance, witnessed by Alice Bouverie and Andrija's wife, Betty, he apparently spoke alternately in English and Ancient Egyptian, writing several pages of hieroglyphics. These were in due course translated and accorded with his vocal utterances. He had apparently been seized by an Ancient Egyptian 'spirit', possibly by 'himself' from a previous incarnation, and he recognised Alice Bouverie as 'Antinea', a priestess or possibly a wife from this former life. Dr Puharich is at pains in relating this, in his book *The Sacred Mushroom*, to be strictly scientific. Harry Stone knew no Ancient Egyptian, and knew nothing of his utterances or writings on emergence from the trance; indeed his trances were a matter of embarrassment to him, and he wanted to lose his capacity for trance as he desired simply to sculpt. However, over a period of the next two years, he was to make a series of remarkable utterances in which he spoke in Ancient Egyptian (this was taped), and wrote extensive hieroglyphics which Egyptologists could decipher.

These writings were always described as coming from 'Ra Ho

Tep'; Puharich refers to their author as the 'Ra Ho Tep personality'. Ra Ho Tep seems to have been a priest of the Egyptian royal family living about 2700 B.C. Their main significance seems to have been a series of statements about 'the plant of life' which is the plant 'with a red crown'. One phrase was translated by an independent Egyptologist as 'Tehuti, it is I who speak, the King, of the beautiful sacred plant of life'. During this particular trance, Stone had drawn a great many mushrooms, and had stated that they contained a drug which killed pain, and facilitated the experience of 'shamanism' or the principle of consciousness existing temporarily outside the body. Puharich concluded that this mushroom was the 'plant of life' referred to in the trance-messages and trance-writings of Harry Stone, and that if it was to have a red cap it must be *Amanita Muscaria*.

In the course of extensive reading on the mushroom which he now undertook, he met Gordon Wasson. Wasson left Mexico City for Huautla and on 29 June 1955, received his initiation into the mushroom rite. 'The curandero', says Puharich, 'offered him the grace of the sacred mushroom, and . . . he was carried into a visionary world where he saw things unknown painted in all the rich and vibrant colour which can only arise within the mind, and not through the eyes, and which has no counterpart in the physical world that human beings ordinarily know'.

The following night, Harry Stone went once more into a trance and, says Puharich, filled eight pages with Egyptian hieroglyphics. 'This is the name of the place of waters from heaven. The purified noble waters. I have made the offering of the noble waters. The waters from heaven from the mouth of the king. My name is the Water from Heaven, waters in an alabaster vessel. In my name of Ren Ho, Waters from Heaven. The alabaster dagger. Cut (or reap) with the noble alabaster dagger. The flowing water from Ra drink it. The noble alabaster dagger. Drink from the place of the flowing waters. The flowing grains. . . .'

Puharich admits that this is obscure but says he regards it as a purification litany indulged in before reaping a magic plant. He now went on an intensive search for the mushroom. He seems to have suspected mysterious or strangely coincidental forces leading him to the many specimens he did find, and which he kept on ice for future use.

On the Atlantic coast he found that the mushroom's life was

short before maggots (surely ecstatic and hallucinating wildly?) destroyed it, as well as other forms of rot.

He tried the mushroom on Harry Stone. Curious events followed rapidly. Stone gave a demonstration of telepathy to Aldous Huxley and unexpectedly slipped into a deep trance. 'In the presence of Aldous and myself,' says Puharich, 'he entered into a dramatic sign-language demonstration whose meaning this time was quite clear to those present. The Ra Ho Tep personality insisted on having the golden mushrooms brought to him.' Puharich obliged. Fetching a mushroom from the ice he placed it in front of the deeply entranced Harry, or rather the Ra Ho Tep personality, who or which became ecstatic over it. He applied the mushroom on his tongue and on the top of his head in ritualistic fashion. Presently the effects of the mushroom started to be felt and he staggered round as though inebriated.

Another man to whom Puharich gave the mushroom said, 'Andrija, I have seen things which I don't believe I could ever describe to you in a million years. I was not here in this room. I don't know where I was. But I was in some far-off place of indescribable beauty. The colours, the forms are beyond description. The only way I can give you an idea of what I saw is that everything around me here is filthy, dirty, and horrible. It looks so ugly here that I hope you don't give me that mushroom too many times; I might not want to come back. I don't know where I was, but I was somewhere outside myself. A woman came to me. I don't know who she was because she could never turn her face to me, and it could all be in the imagination. The woman guided me and took me I don't know where. I don't know whether I was walking or flying or what. I never had this before so I can't describe it. We came to a land. I didn't see any trees. I can't say that, but I did see flowers. I can't describe them. They were so beautiful. I saw houses; there were many many houses. The only thing that I can tell you about the houses is that they all looked like cupolas, they were like beehives. They were round and all with beautiful colours. I know that where my mind was is real. Its beauty is beyond description. And this world is so ugly. I'm sorry I came back.'

These rhapsodies were found to be utterly uncharacteristic of the man, who was held to be 'essentially unintoxicated and sensible'.

As my researches continued I was learning that, if nothing else, extraordinary things happen to people who research into the magic mushroom.

A magic mushroom is also the subject of Professor Allegro's famous *The Sacred Mushroom and the Cross*.

He says, 'The mushroom has always been a thing of mystery. The ancients were troubled by its manner of growth without seed, the speed with which it made its appearance after rain and its as rapid disappearance. Born from a volva or 'egg' it appears like a small penis, raising itself like the human organ sexually aroused, and when it spread wide its canopy the old botanists saw it as a phallus bearing the 'burden' of a woman's groin. Every aspect of the mushroom's existence was fraught with sexual allusions and in its phallic form the ancients saw a replica of the fertility god himself. It was the 'Son of God' its drug was a purer form of God's own spermatozoa than that discoverable in any other form of living matter. It was, in fact, God himself, manifest on earth. To the mystic it was a divinely given means of entering heaven; God had come down in the flesh to show the way to Himself, by Himself.'

Later, Allegro says that the whole story of the Garden of Eden and what took place in it is in fact, 'mushroom-based mythology, not least in the identity of the "tree" as the sacred fungus. . . . Even as late as the thirteenth century some recollection of the old tradition was known amongst Christians, to judge from the fresco painted on the wall of an old ruined church in Plaincoualt in France. There the *Amanita Muscaria* is gloriously portrayed, entwined with a serpent, whilst Eve stands by, holding her belly.'

Allegro speaks of man's early sense of his helplessness in the face of nature and a hostile world around him. 'Somehow man had to establish communications with the source of the world fertility, and thereafter maintain a right relationship with it. Over the course of time he built up a body of experimental knowledge of rituals that he or his representatives could perform, or words to recite.

'If the rain in the desert lands were the source of life, then the moisture from heaven must be only a more abundant kind of spermatozoa. If the male organ ejaculated this precious fluid and made life in the woman, then above the skies the source of nature's semen must be a mighty penis, as the earth which bore its offspring was the womb.

'It follows therefore that to induce the heavenly phallus to complete its orgasm, man must stimulate it by sexual means, by singing,
by dancing, orgiastic displays and, above all, by the performance
of the copulatory act itself.'

One result of this, he says, would be that 'the penis in the sky
would rise and spurt its vital juice when man commanded.'

And his book is an attempt to show that 'Judaism and Christianity
are such cultic expressions of this endless pursuit by man to discover instant power, knowledge.

'To raise the crops the farmer copulated with his wife in the fields.
To seek the drug that would send his soul winging to the seventh
heaven and back, the initiates into the religious mysteries have
their priestesses seduce the god and draw him into their clasp as
a woman fascinates her partner's penis to erection.

'For the way to God and the fleeting view of heaven was through
plants more plentifully endued with the sperm of God than any
other. These were the drug herbs, the science of whose cultivation
and use have been accumulated over centuries of observation and
dangerous experiment.

'Very rarely, and then only for urgent and practical purposes,
were their secrets ever committed to writing. Normally they would
be passed from the priest to the initiate by word of mouth.'

But, if for some drastic reason it did become necessary to write
down the precious names of the herbs and the manner of their use,
it would have to be in some esoteric form.

'Such an occasion we believe was the Jewish revolt of A.D. 66.
Instigated probably by members of the cult, swayed by their drug
induced madness to believe God had called them to master the world
in His name, they provoked the mighty powers of Rome to swift
and terrible action. Jerusalem was ravaged, her temple destroyed.
Judaism was disrupted.'

He says that information about the magic mushroom was pre-
served for history as follows : by telling 'the story of a rabbi called
Jesus, and investing him with the power and names of the magic
drug. To have him live before the terrible events that had disrupted
their lives, to preach a love between men, extending even to the
hated Romans. Thus, reading such a tale, should it fall into Roman
hands, even their mortal enemies might be deceived and not probe
farther into the activities of the cells of the mystery cults within
their territory.'

The ruse, he says, failed. Christians, hated and despised, were hauled forth and slayed in their thousands.

In an article by Robert Graves I was intrigued to find the following, 'In Scotland amanita and whisky are taken together by certain poachers. The mixture is called a "cathie", supposedly in memory of Catherine the Great of Russia, who fancied it.'

Wasson says, 'The Fly Agaric (*Amanita Muscaria*) is unique amongst the psychotropic plants in one of its properties : it is an inebriant in *two forms.*

'*First Form :*

'Taken directly, and by directly I mean by eating the raw mushroom or by drinking its juice squeezed out and taken neat, or mixed with water, or with water and milk or curds, and perhaps barley in some form, and honey; also mixed with herbs such as epilobium.

'*Second Form :*

'Taken in the urine of the person who has ingested the fly agaric in the first form.'

Robert Graves comments on the above passage, 'What he is saying here is that when the mushroom juice is squeezed out and drunk only some of the indoles which induce hallucinations pass from the stomach into the blood stream; the rest lodge in the kidneys and there mix with the urine. The urine is filtered through sheep's wool, and then drunk mixed with milk or curd.

'Not only the Palaeosiberians and a small Mongol enclave in Afghanistan . . . use these two methods. So, apparently, do certain Lapps and Finns, who are said to filter and get high on the urine of reindeer that have eaten the *Amanita Muscaria.*' The fact of the mushroom being drunk in people's urine is, so Graves says, recalled in a story about Indra, the thunder god mentioned in the Rig Veda.

Indra, so it is said, was once asked by his worshippers for a taste of soma, the divine food of the gods. He unwillingly promised it to them. Presently a stinking and diseased beggar appeared.

'Come and drink my piss,' the beggar whined. They drove him away. When later they reverently asked Indra to keep his promise, he answered, 'I offered you some and you refused it.'

Graves and Wasson, in an article printed in the *Atlantic Monthly*, asserted that Dionysus, the Greek god, represented the intoxication produced by *Amanita Muscaria*. It has also been suggested that ambrosia, the food of the Greek gods, was also none other than the magic mushroom. One reason given for this was that Dionysus' annual festival, the Ambrosia, fell in the Autumn mushroom picking season.

Wasson's *Soma, Food of the Gods,* proposed that soma derives from the *Amanita Muscaria,* and that the mushroom was imported into India in the second millenium, B.C., from the birch forests of the high Himalayas.

The autobiography of Joan Grant tells how she had a vision in which she saw the *Amanita Muscaria* in sacred use amongst the Pharoahs of ancient Egypt.

It has also been reported that sacrificial victims in Mayan ceremonies were treated as gods before their ritual murder. They were allowed to mate with virgins whose lives had been organised to lead up to just such a happy event.

The sacrificial victims were intoxicated, so says Alan Klein, probably with the *Psilocybe* mushroom. 'It appears that the Mayan priesthood regulated the taking of the mushroom. It could be that those priests in the highest positions in the Mayan hierarchy were entitled to the mushroom several times in their lives.'

Klein writes, 'Various myths have been created that centre around a mushroom. One of the most interesting is the creation myth of the islanders of the Admiralty Islands in the South Pacific. It is told here that "When the sea had dried so that men appeared, the first two beings, after planting trees and creating food plants, made two mushrooms. The first man threw one of the mushrooms high into the sky, creating the moon, while the first woman tossed the other mushroom upward and formed the sun." ' (R. B. Dixon, *Mythology of all Races,* New York, 1964, vol. 9, p. 111.)

'The hallucinogenic mushroom can be traced in the myth of Soma, the god-plant of the Hindu Vedas. It should be noted that R. G. Wasson and Robert Graves have linked Soma to the sacred mushroom. Gladys M. N. Davis in *The Asiatic Dionysos* successfully identified the Greek Dionysos with Soma. We have here the vital link between the mysticism of the mushroom in the East and its arrival in the West. It should be noted that the Greek myth of Dionysos has him travelling to India, conquering India, teaching the art of wine-making there, and returning to Europe with his wild party of raving Maenads, who tore calves limb from limb in their rituals, rituals which have been reported to be held under the influence of *Amanita Muscaria.*

'But let us turn our attention to Soma and try to perceive some of its myth and mysteries.

'According to the texts of the ancient Vedas, immortality could be achieved either by ascetic practice or by drinking Soma. Indra, the most popular of the Vedic gods, talks of having drunk himself into intoxication with Soma. The Rig Veda, one of the sacred texts, contains mostly hymns used in the Soma ritual.

'Soma, the Avestan Haoma (meaning "the pressed juice"), is the deity of the whole of the ninth book of the Rig Veda.

'The plant itself produced, when its stems and caps were pressed, a juice which after careful straining was offered, pure or with the addition of sour milk, to the gods and drunk by the priests. The colour was brown and ruddy, and, frequently, mention is made of the stones by which it was pounded, though it seems also to have been produced by mortar and pestle, as was common among the parsis. If Soma is passed through a filter or strainer it is referred to as paramána ("flowing clear"). Besides sour milk, natural milk or barley water were commonly added, and hence Soma is lord of the waters, who makes the rain to steam from the heaven. The waters are his sisters, and he is the embryo or child of the waters. The sound of the juice as it flows is likened to thunder, its swiftness (of action) to that of steel.'

From Volume 6 of *Mythology of All Races:*

'The exhilarating power of Soma doubtless explains his divinity. It is a plant which confers powers beyond the natural, and the Soma is the draught of immortality (amorta), the ambrosia. The gods love it; it gives them immortality no less than it gives it to man, and one hymn depicts the ecstasy of feeling produced in Indra by the drink, which makes him feel able to dispose of the earth at his pleasure. Soma is also rich in healing and lord of the plants. When quaffed, he stimulates speech and is the lord of speech. He is a maker of seers, a protector of prayer, and his wisdom is extolled. He gazes with wisdom on man and so has a thousand eyes. The great deeds of the gods owe their success to their drinking the Soma. It is mentioned, for example, that Indra filled three lakes with Soma for himself to drink before the slaying of Vitra. When drunk by Indra, Soma makes the Sun to rise in the sky. There is also identification of the moon with Soma.'

Ten years ago at Guernavaca, south of Mexico City, Dr Timothy Leary, a Harvard psychotherapist, ate some mushrooms that he had bought from a witch-doctor in a nearby village. It was a sunny afternoon beside the swimming pool of his rented holiday villa, and within a few minutes he felt himself, 'being swept over the edge of a sensory Niagara into a maelstrom of transcendental visions and hallucinations. The next five hours could be described in many extravagant metaphors, but it was above all and without question the deepest religious experience of my life.' It was thus that the American high-priest of the psychedelic, the great 'turner-on' of American youth, was himself first turned on; with far-reaching results.

Leary vowed 'to dedicate the rest of my life as a psychologist to the systematic exploration of this new instrument.' He was committed to healing, and he was convinced that psychedelic drugs could cure not only those obviously ill, but the whole of 'sick middle-aged materialistic tired power-seeking America'. He revolted then and there against the entire fabric of American-Christian-Western-civilisation-consciousness. His purchases from the American witch-doctor gave him something which he thought infinitely deeper, truer, richer, more beautiful and holy than allowed in the normal outlets and activities of the society in which he was living, a society tired and sick at heart, committed to prosperity and war. He enunciated the doctrine 'turn on, tune in, drop out'. Even if he could not hope to convince the 'menopausal' power-loving establishment to drop their obscene games of politics, business, and militarism, and discover the beauty and elation of inward explora-tion, he was convinced that enough young people follow-ing his gospel of the psychedelic reorientation would in fact vitally change American society as a whole. He was soon to discover LSD.

Richard Evans Schultes in two lectures originally published in the *Texas Journal of Pharmacy II (1961)* says, 'Sahagun, a Span-ish friar, was one of the first Europeans to refer to *teo-nanacatl*' (an Indian word for the sacred mushroom). He made several refer-ences to mushrooms 'which are harmful and intoxicating like wine' so that those who eat of them 'see visions, feel a faintness of heart and are provoked to lust'. He detailed the effects in one reference saying that the natives ate them with honey and 'when they begin

to be excited by them start dancing, singing, weeping. Some,'
Sahagun continued, 'do not want to sing but sit down . . . and see
themselves dying in a vision; others see themselves being eaten by
a wild beast; others imagine that they are capturing prisoners of
war or, they are rich, and they possess many slaves, that they had
committed adultery and were to have their heads crushed for the
offence . . . and when the drunken state had passed, they talk over
amongst themselves the visions which they have seen.'

He continues, 'There are four or five references to the sacred
fungi in these early writings. According to Tezozomoc, for example,
inebriating mushrooms were part of the coronation feast of
Montezuma in 1502. Friar Motolinia, who died in 1569, mentioned the sacred psychotomemetic mushrooms in a work on pagan
rites and idolatries. The physician, Hernandez, who studied the
medicinal law of Mexican natives for seven years, spoke of three
kinds of mushroom used as narcotics and worshipped. Of some,
called *teyhuinti*, he wrote that they, "cause not death but madness
that on occasion is lasting, of which the symptom is a kind of un-
controlled laughter . . . these are deep yellow, acrid and of a not
displeasing freshness. There are others again which, without
inducing laughter, bring before the eyes all kinds of things, such as
wars, and the likeness of demons. Yet others there are not less
desired by princes for their festivals and banquets, and these fetch
a high price. With night long vigils are they sought, awesome and
terrifying. This kind is tawny and somewhat acrid." The following
mushrooms make up the Wasson-Heim list of Mexican hallucin-
ogens, *Canatharellaceae-Conocybe Siliginoides*, growing on dead
tree trunks; *Strobhariaceae-Psilocybe Mexicana*, a small tawny
inhabitant of wet pastures, apparently the most highly prized by
the users; *Psylocybe Zapotecorum* of marshy ground and known
by the Zacotecs as "crown of thorns mushroom"; *Psylocybe
Caerulescens Car. Mazatecorum*, the so-called "landslide mushroom" which grows on decaying sugar cane refuse; *Psylocybe
Caerelluescens Var. Nigripes*, that have a native name meaning
"mushroom of superior reason"; and *Stropharia Cubensis*.

'Undoubtedly there were many tribes in ancient Mexico who
employed *teo-nanacate* (the word means flesh of the gods), but we
know of certainty only of the Chichimecas, who spoke nahuatl. We
know that today the sacred mushrooms are consumed by the
Mazatecs, Ghinantecs, Chatinox, Zacotecs, Mixtecs, and Mijes, all

of Oaxaca; by the Nohoahs of Mexico; and possibly by the Tarascans of Michoacan and the Otomics of Puebla.'

Of the Oaxacan mushrooms Schultes says that the most important is *Psilocybe Mexicana*. 'Beside the kaleidoscopic play of visual hallucinations in colour, the outstanding symptoms of psilocybe intoxication are; muscular relaxation, flaccidity and midriosis early in narcosis, followed by a period of emotional disturbance, such as extreme hilarity and difficulty in concentration. It is at this point that the visual and auditory hallucinations appear, eventually to be followed by lassitude and mental and physical depression, with serious alteration of time and space perception. One peculiarity of the narcosis which promises to be of interest in experimental psychiatry is the isolation of the subject from the world around him – that is, without a loss of consciousness, he is rendered completely indifferent to his environment, which becomes unreal to him as his dream-like state becomes real.'

What is the connection between the hallucinatory mushrooms of Mexico and the version most frequently found in the Western world – *Amanita Muscaria*?

The connection appears to be that certain mushrooms are hallucinatory in effect, hence magical, and the *Amanita* is the form in which these are usually found in the Western world, while those mentioned above are the forms in which it is usually found in Mexico.

Alan Klein writes, '*The Psilocybe Mexicana* is an edible hallucinogenic species of mushroom belonging to the brown spore group of the family of *Agaricaceae* fungi, in which the white spored *Amanita Muscaria* is also found. The family of *Agaricaceae* is subdivided into five groups according to the colour of the spore of the mushroom.'

Why is it that the *Amanita Muscaria*, with its huge red surface flecked with white spots, so often forms the seat for gnomes? Was it because partaking of the *Amanita Muscaria* enabled authors to catch sight of these creatures? Was *Amanita* the mushroom that Alice nibbled before she went through the looking glass? There is reason to think that Lewis Carrol had read of a hallucinatory mushroom shortly before he wrote his book.* What of the numerous stone statues of mushrooms, most of them roughly a foot high,

* In 'British Fungi' from the *Gardeners Chronicle and Agricultural Gazette* by M. C. Cooke (October 1862).

which are so frequently found in the highland of Guatemala which, Wasson says, do indeed represent mushrooms and are the symbol of a religion flourishing about 1500 B.C.? Or were they merely vermin proof supports for buildings such as can still be seen under some old British wooden barns?

Obviously there have been other hallucinatory agents at large in the world beside the mushroom. And taking all these together, is it not worth asking how much in the mind of man that is fabled or strange, how much of religious or fairy tale or daemon-like fancies, how much of the stuff of poetry, how many dreams that troubled or made ecstatic the questing minds of scholars, mystics, holy men – how much of these could have existed if it were not for the magic mushroom?

One way of classifying the civilisation of a country is by asking how they get high, what intoxicants they use. The *tulla* of Ethiopia (which has to be newly brewed every three days and is the colour of grey mud) gives, so I have heard, a rapid and lovely quality to the nature. It is I think clear that beer-drinking nations like Britain, Germany, America, have different natures to those nations that primarily drink wine.

Mexicans have *pulche* – that milk-like intoxicating drink of the cactus. They have tequila. But beyond that they have the magic mushroom.

Can it be that those swinging qualities of Mexico, that joy, that irrationality, many of those things I loved about it – can it be that these qualities too were contributed to this country from the cap of the worshipped sacred magic mushroom?

9

Jungle Temple of Palenque

We are flying over the unkempt wide hills above San Cristobal de las Casas, watching the evening fall, watching the dark clouds massing around a bright patch of sky, their fleecy edges like lace, seeing the clouds lit intermittently by the purple blank flash of lightning and from the town the shine of the occasional bright illumination of neon.

I am flying in a four-seater plane over the empty hills to Palenque, passing the occasional straw-roofed village stranded far beneath us, seeing where these villages lie down there, approached by straggling strands of roads. Sometimes we are close to the mountains and the peaks stick up suddenly sharp below us, the trees sticking up so steeply that one might think they would pierce the belly of the aircraft, then dropping back again until they are far beneath us.

I see Palenque below me now, that mysterious Mayan ruin which like so many others lies mostly impenetrably lost amidst the jungle, the sweet-smelling fetid jungle. Nature is wanton in these parts, and as always the jungle grips me and excites me.

The extent of Palenque, slowly entwined and covered in the steady march and stealthy approach of the jungle, has never been established. Its size has been variously estimated as sixty miles, ten times the size of New York, or three times the size of London. More likely it is four or five miles in each direction.

Only the centre of the city has been excavated. All the rest is impenetrable green darkness. At the front of it is a structure like a slabbed pyramid which stretches up into the sky, immensely high. A notice says, 'Tumba Abierta de 11 a 12'. Pagoda-like structures rise up against a background of trees into whose glossy, dusky depths the light scarcely penetrates.

To the outer casements of these temples there adhere stones which are the remains of yet larger edifices, peeled off like the skin of a tangerine. I enter an endless series of these terrifying catacombs. I nearly slip and fall. Now through the immense darkness of the subterranean chamber I peer out through a chink to see stone steps rise up, decked with green fern-like lichen. To one of the ancient walls sticks a butterfly with phosphorescent orange wings.

Some beautiful young Americans pass by on horses which, although it's only the start of their journey, are bloody and scarred and wasted with disease. They say that they are going to stay in an Indian village.

A vein of water runs through the midst of these ruins, cool amidst the blinding heat. Horses stand tethered. I climb down into the water and now I am in the subterranean depths of a concealed channel that runs far beneath the ruins, cool after the sweaty heat of the jungle.

From the central platform of these lofty, appallingly high edifices, I look out over the endless jungle. And here are lists of dates, a sort of calendar but on a vast scale, the meanest interval being twenty years.

Up at this great height it was discovered recently that what had the appearance of a vast chunk of stone floor was not really a floor. The design of a snake didn't stop at floor level but seemed to continue down beneath it.

Excavations began and archaeologists discovered a staircase stretching down beneath the stones, going down for an immense distance in such a way as to suggest that at some time those who had control of the city, probably when they were abandoning it, decided to make it as difficult as possible for anyone ever to go again down this passage. They began to dig, and it took them something like twelve months before the last of the rubble was removed.

At one point when they thought they had reached the bottom at last, the steps gave an abrupt turn and continued in another direction for as far as they had already gone.

At another point there were narrow window shafts through the immensely wide walls of the pyramid leading to the outside air. Alongside the staircase ran the body of the snake, connecting life at the top with whatever lay buried underneath. At the foot of the stairs, descending through the pyramid to practically ground level, they discovered treasure – clay dishes, shells filled with red paint, beads and jewellery and a narrow space, far underground, which contained the bodies of five or six young men – 'in a very poor condition'.

Was this the end of their quest? No. They came upon a gigantic slab of stone, cut so as to fit exactly the shape of the passage. With fantastic exertion they worked to shift this great stone. And inside saw what it had been intended that no one would ever see again – a large vaulted chamber in the very heart of the pyramid. The steps inside were jagged, not worn very soft, and glistening with moisture. Here there was a vast slab weighing many tons, and decorated with intricate designs of a rather psychedelic appearance. A figure, legs raised, lay back on a couch in a curious position as if balancing an extraordinary edifice on top of him. The centre of gravity seems to shift as you look at it.

The whole place was filled with stalactites and, when these had been broken, inside this fantastic sarcophagus ten feet long, seven feet broad, was found the body of a tall man between forty and fifty years of age. The man was decorated with jade ornaments. He wore a diadem of jade discs. His ears were stopped with several pieces of jade representing a flower, and many necklaces, made mainly of jade. He also wore rings, and a jade mask made of mosaic – an incredible sculpture, a product of what at that moment can seem to the viewer a wonderful religion that has at its heart not some twisted figure of doom, but a God of Joy.

The edifices of Palenque were later used for shelters by peasants, who left evidence of their stay there in the form of many grinding stones amongst the ruins. Little by little the peasants too were unable to resist the encroachment of the jungle as it slowly crept through the metropolis, overwhelming the buildings. They also left. Behind the pyramids the jungle is noisy, its discordant notes blaring and buzzing like tin trumpets. Giant dragon-flies are buzzing around, and birds make curious hooting noises. A green snake slides himself sinisterly, tail up, among the rocks. The spot has become a bathing place for the neighbouring towns, and girls in ill-fitting one-piece bathing dresses are wading about in the water.

It is good to be back among people again. The remoteness and strangeness of those old Mayan ruins is terrifying.

As I go out, I see that at the entrance to the ruins of Palenque the horse of one of the Americans has collapsed onto the ground.

Efforts to raise it are useless. One of them will have to walk.

I walk down to a little place that advertises itself as a restaurant on a crudely daubed notice at the side of the road in the midst of the jungle. I find myself on a mean thatched terrace, open to the jungle on all sides. Here there flourish the vast shapes of cactus and of palm, but there's no food, only a promise of frijoles (fried beans) later. I get talking to a good-looking blonde American who was present at the first opening of the tomb.

She says, 'For months and months we toiled away removing the rubble down these stairs, and when we finally got to the bottom we found a stone door, we couldn't get it open, it had been sealed with an extraordinary form of seal, to this day we don't know what it was. We used every possible device to get it open. Finally, we poured acid on it. Then, with crowbars, hatchets, everything that you can conceive, we at last got it open. And I will never forget what we saw inside. The entire sepulchre, as it now is, was filled with stalactites glimmering in the light of the torch, incredibly beautiful. In those early hours, every move destroyed great beauty. It was a terrible thing to have to break them. But we had to do it in order to unearth the stone with its lovely hieroglyphics and pictures.

'The central tower in the middle of Palenque is a fake. There's no proof that the top of its roof looked like that. I pointed this out to the man who built it and he said, yes, but in ten years in this climate it will look like all the rest, and who's going to know the difference?

'You can see the same thing in the attitude of many people to the modern village of Palenque. It had a lot of things which were quite charming – thatched palapas down either side of the road, a church at the end, a delightful and pastoral scene. But they destroyed every bit of it. They put up corrugated iron roofs on top of the old palapas, and they put up a lot of extremely ugly signs.'

On the way back the plane passed through various turbulent rainstorms. I gazed down on the farms far underneath, each with its own clearing in the midst of the jungle, as much as a man and his family could work, little circles cut out from the jungle, and then the vast trees again. Some of the more outlying farms seemed to have been abandoned, the vegetation having encroached until it totally engulfed them.

10

Horrors in Gilded Cases

The day begins early, before it is light, with the sporadic explosion of rockets. For some days before, as if in anticipation, there have been outbursts of gunfire-like bangs. The cockerels start their crowing early. Then, prompt at 5.30 a.m., comes the frantic banging of bells.

I look up from the valley to the church where it stands up on the hill, surrounded by two or three sparse little trees. The air is limpid, blue, with tiny patches of white cloud. The steps leading up to the church are already thronged with people. And, as another blast of fireworks shatters the morning air, I think how far this all seems from Britain with its smug late risings and complaints about church bells.

Yet more rockets are rising from the hills, and the church now is entirely enveloped in smoke, as if it had become the seat of violent warfare. Four men are engaged in hurling rockets into the air. Somebody has swarmed up a telegraph pole in order to wave a flag and there come the sounds of sundry tootings and pipings, restless music emanating from Mariachis at the top of the hill.

A man is cutting at the foliage with a long machete to make it look better for the people who are climbing up on this day of pilgrimage. At the top now I can see four men who, by a little improvised fire at which they light them, are hurling home-made rockets into the sky. Sometimes they hurl them piecemeal, one after the other, sometimes all simultaneously in a deafening blast. The rockets appear to be home-made, long sticks at the top of which bits of type-written paper have been closely bound with string. From the top of the hill I look down now on the prison. People are sitting out in the exercise yard, and, at the main door of the prison, their friends and relatives are queuing to bring them food.

It's just an ordinary fiesta. Around the church there are tables covered with plastic or pink and yellow towels laid out with bananas, fruit, shortcake, and glasses of atole, a warm liquid made from oatmeal. The band set up their instruments outside the back of the church. From inside comes raucous singing.

The smoke now is billowing out from the rockets, billowing over a couple of buxom pretty girls who run away, giggling, pulling their lace mantillas over their heads. The men who fire the rockets carry on with their job with the gravity of people engaged in vital deeds of warfare.

Now the priest emerges from his church, dressed in black, with a golden cross with which he advances to the edge of the hill, followed by stragglers. He raises the golden cross, serious faced, and blesses the valley. There is a little boy with him ringing a bell frenziedly, and another little boy with an incense burner, wafting out great gusts and wafts of incense. Now they turn and return into the church.

In the valley I can see water-drenched grass from which trees sprout. Vast wide pastures sprinkled with grazing cattle. A horse pawing at that bright water.

Marc Chadourne, in his book *Anahuac*, tells how in a village in Tabasco the local saint had stopped working miracles. No longer did he produce rain or cure diseases. No amount of praying had any effect. Then one of the Indians hit on a solution. From a nearby market he brought back a little St Teresa, a delicate and pretty statue. They placed her beside the saint where he stood in the church. And not long after that, the rain began and people were once again cured.

In another church, every morning a sacristan was amazed to find that a statue of the Virgin Mary had moved, ending up alongside the local male saint in his niche, although the night before they had been placed well apart. The sacristan tried glue and screws. Still no luck, the Virgin persistently ended up in the niche beside the saint. Finally, resolving to put an end for good to these tricks, the sacristan shut up the Virgin in a chest and slept on top of it. It is a puzzle to know what the sacristan's true attitude to the Virgin was.

The government only allows a certain number of priests. It

tolerates the Church but doesn't encourage it. In the old revolutionary days, there were bitter feuds between Church and State, and priests, carrying the banner of Christ, used to ransack trains and perform armed robberies. The country is still fairly confused about religion. For instance, prostitutes wear round their necks the medallion of the Virgin of Solitude, who, it is said, protects them against venereal disease.

Madame de la Barca, writing in the last century, says, 'When the organ ceased playing, the church was suddenly plunged into profound darkness. Out of the gloom came a terrible voice, crying, "My brothers, when Christ was bound by the Jews they scourged Him". Immediately we heard the sound of hundreds of lashes falling on naked flesh. I cannot conceive anything more horrible, the noise grew more terrifying every minute. Incredible though this may seem the horrible penance went on. From time to time a special groan could be heard and occasionally the voice of a monk encouraging them with exclamations or short passages of scripture. . . .'

At one time a large number of pious frauds were discovered – such as a Virgin Mary in Mexico City whose eyes rolled according to the dictates of hidden bits of string worked by concealed monks, or a Christ that sweated continuously as a result of a coating of melted salt.

We are going on a tour of churches. My hair sprinkled with confetti from fiestas, my feet plunged in the mud of streets without drains, reeling from tequila, my senses drugged with the fumes of incense, I am driving with two American girls. The car is perpetually getting stuck on the heavy ruts of the road. We pass an old church with brick-made domes, and stop to explore a cloister overgrown with green grass. Outside the cloister there is a farm, the little yard fenced in with organ cactus, a little pig, a vast bull with a great bulge in his black neck. Inside an adobe hut nearby I hear the sound of slapping. A child pounding out tortillas. Two gleamingly white goats are eating corn from the lid of a huge tin, one of them on his delicate knees. Another cow is tied to an organ cactus. And behind the little farm the red land stretches away to the vast mountain on which stand ruins.

This church is fantastic, filled with monsters in glass cases, and on the ceiling of the nave endless paintings of cherubs, men hanging upside down, headless men holding their heads in their arms with bishops' crowns on their heads.

The last great Mexican revolution took place just before the Russian revolution. Hoards of Indian Peons, having been deprived of their lands by the Diaz regime, rose, and, led by the famous Zapata, these starving men fought, razed haciendas to the ground and marched on Mexico City. Nine months before the first guarantees of the Soviets, the Mexican working-class proletariat had been promised a complete redistribution of lands and the restoration of their communal property. Frescoes of that date by Diego Riviera and others show the red flag of Russia and that of Mexico flying side by side. And, until that time, many priests' mitres had been literally covered with diamonds, ribbed with gold and studded with jewels, and many of their vessels had been pure gold.

An Englishman, H. L. G. Ward, tells how in the mining districts each miner at the end of a week's work had to give the Church one real, about a pound, for his forthcoming funeral. One priest refused to bury a man's son because he was behind in his payment. The man said, 'But what shall I do with the body?'

To which the priest replied, 'Salt it and eat it.'

The opposition of the Church towards any reform has been quite astounding. Most recent of all attempted revolutions was in 1926, when the Archbishop of Mexico publicly repudiated the constitution. This was the time when armed bands, some of them led by priests, ran the country. In 1927 two trains were attacked and pillaged by gangs led by priests. They massacred guards, railwaymen and travellers, and burnt alive a dozen women and twenty children.

'In the name of God, your loving Father,' said a popular leader of those days, 'you have been beaten, bruised and wounded. In the name of Jesus, meek and mild, you have been oppressed and enslaved and deprived of your homes and lands. And now in the name of the devil, as the priests call our revolution, your homes and lands and families are given back to you.' And the mob cried back with a single voice, 'Viva el diablo.'

We wander on through the church, seeing beatific saints enclosed in gilded glass cases. In another case a monstrous figure of a man is being burnt with plaster flames, and he kisses where the flames touch his flesh. And beyond this, there is a dark-skinned saint, and in front of the altar an Indian is kneeling with his two little children deep in prayer, his arms outstretched in a gesture of abandon.

There are flowers, both plastic and real. Another saint, his limbs scarred and stained with blood, is staggering forward with a dog at his heels. Candles are burning in front of the saints and before one statue is a brandy glass filled with liquid wax and a taper burning at its top. The walls are decorated with murals. At the back is a door of green glass. At the altar there are silken hangings, endlessly leading onwards until beneath the East window, Christ, again in a glass case, stretches out His hands in benediction.

The church is filled with birds who zoom backwards and forwards across the aisle. There is another glass case, occupied at the moment by no saint, but containing faded flowers which somebody has absent-mindedly left. In another glass case a saint lies prostrate, covered in velvet and trinkets. Here is a glass case occupied by Christ dressed in an old sheet with rudimentary lacework down the side. There is an oleograph of the Virgin holding up Christ in the air, and another oleograph of a Virgin holding a heart with a sword thrust through it up in the air. Both her feet are sprinkled with shiny gold tinsel. The church is vast and white and empty of pews. And always there is the chirruping of deftly flying birds.

There are very few candles. At one point there is half a Super-Mex Motor Oil tin which has been perforated, filled with oil and given a wick. The altar is cascading down with artificial flowers and candles, and hangings stamped with silver paper.

Wandering on through the church I see saints with real eyelashes and glass eyes. Christ makes yet one more final appearance, the blood streaming down His face from His crown of thorns on His head, real human hair, His bloody dripping hands stretched up on the cross above Him. Another saint has a real hatchet in his hand, a dagger sticking into his side, a holy book under his arm and in his other hand a tin cup with a flower in it. The harmonium in this church has a cover that buttons down its front and over its legs with pearly buttons.

The Swimming Tank

By day Mexican children sport endlessly in these bright waters. By night the baths are the domain of visiting Gringos, who rent huts beside the water and come here to smoke pot and exchange anecdotes.

The waters are very dark, coursing through the tank, gushing out at the further end. And this little hut contains two beds on which recline various Gringos, all high on ardiente or hashish.

Outside, beyond the terrace, is a room of immense length containing long tables on which stand a large quantity of candles burning brightly in the darkness, brightly lit for no one. One of the Gringos who is giving the party is letting off fireworks, holding rockets in his hand and lighting their ends with little fireworks. The rockets go soaring from his hands into the sky. Both of these Gringos wear ancient garments, and at their waists gleam machetes.

One of the girls here is called Fifi, she is part French, and is frilly, pert, full of shrieks and exclamation marks, arch, coy. She says that she's married to a wealthy man in Mexico City whom she doesn't love. She's got a child by him and for this reason will never leave him. She says, 'My own father left me, and that's made me unhappy. I want to make sure that at any rate my boy is all right. But I'm bored. You like me? Isn't it warm? Would you like to change? Would you like me to come to your apartment so that you can take a shower?'

'The sulpur pools are good,' says a dark American. 'They're about two miles from here – we could go there in my car.'

'What are the sulphur pools?' I ask.

'It's a place where natural springs of hot water come streaming out of the earth, surrounded by grey and fetid mud, in a clearing which is entirely bamboos. The scene is fantastic, and there you'll see how I work,' he added quietly. We pile into his car and I sit next to the girl who attracts me. All the time that we drive she excites me by high-pitched shrieks.

She says, 'After the sulphur pools, will you make love to me?'

'Yes, of course.'

The sulphur pools are even more marvellous than the dark American described them. Lit by a single low-wattage hanging bulb, the steamy torrents of caliginous water come pouring out from a pipe in the midst of bamboos which, immensely high and dense in this area, are caked with a thick grey alluvial deposit. The water plunges down headlong into its pool from a rusty pipe and the bamboos stand up around as if guarding a secret place. Steam rises up around us into the air and the place has an unreal and haunted quality, increased by the presence of floating frogs. I pull off my clothes and plunge into the water with exuberance.

I hurl myself back and forwards through the water, plunging now underneath and now over the top of the tepid seductive fluid which is criss-crossed with currents of different strengths and different heats of water. All the time I am thinking of the time to come with Fifi. But, unknown to me, Fifi has already found her man. There in the midst of the sulphur pool, beneath a vast falling jet, deranged out of her senses by the tepid seductiveness of the water, all sense of value now lost, she is already making love to the dark American.

Mexicans admire, yet hate the Gringos. They hate many Gringos for using Mexico as a gigantic bedroom. But there is perhaps a certain amount of double-think in their attitude.

'Do you speak English?' asks the boss in an advertisement outside a Language School.

And the smarmy American-style young Mexican replies, with a smile, says, 'Yes sir, I speak, write, and read English.'

'The post is certainly secure now,' comments the advertisement.

The Coca-colarisation of Mexico has stretched far. The walls of even the most primitive earth-floored cafes have their Coca-cola signs – often of a blazing sexuality. One shows a young girl romping with two sailors, her pinky-white petticoat zooming up in the air around her white thighs, and there are three girls and two men sitting round watching, one of the men is holding up a Coke bottle at an oblique angle and the girls are amazed, delighted, quite astonished, turned on at the sight of this bottle of Coke the man

An Indian village

Piazza of an Indian village

Watching cattle by Lake Chapala

An Indian family washing

is holding out to show them. This poetry, this Coca-lyricism, stretches into the furthest areas of Mexico that I penetrated.

In the most distant parts of the jungle where one imagined oneself to be many hours ride from the nearest road, it is not uncommon to meet the lurching form of the Coca-cola lorry.

At one time the Coca-cola people seem to have handed out free refrigerators, for reasons possibly known to themselves, to anyone who asked. In one village I went to in the jungle practically every earth-floored palapa had got incorporated in its architecture somewhere a defunct Coca-cola refrigerator. Why they were issued in the first place is a mystery, since no ice is available in these parts, and there is no electricity. Often they are used as tables.

Hen houses are another popular use for the refrigerators. At one house, a little hut outside which a smarter than usual Coca-cola refrigerator stood, I went in and asked the lady for a Coke. 'Yes, yes, of course,' she cried. 'Sit down, sit down here.' She brought out the only chair for me to sit on and placed it on a flat part of the floor. Then she dispatched a little child to go to some apparently distant place and buy a bottle of Coca-cola. I looked about me There was little decoration in the hut other than a toothbrush heavily clogged with toothpaste, stuck into a crevice of the reed walls. A candle in a box hung from rope tied to a beam in the middle of the roof. Distantly outside in the hot dusty village I could hear the sounds of Mariachis singing.

I sat a while on my chair and at length the boy returned with a bottle of Coke. He poured it out into an old tooth-mug. From under the chair on which I was sitting came the sound of a hen cackling to itself. I smiled at this, I hadn't heard the bird enter or noticed it sitting there. The lady was hovering about, bustling, dusting, behaving in the way that she felt the proprietor of a café should behave. When she heard the chirping clucking noise of the hen beneath my chair she smiled benignly. 'Ah,' she said, 'you are wondering what that sound is. I'll tell you. It is the radio!'

The Mexicans mainly seemed to like me. But that is perhaps because I am not American.

One American girl said to me, 'The sheer pettiness of it is what I find hard to understand. I can understand that they might hate us rationally because we invaded them and took much of their land. But that they can feel this searing unreasoning intensity of emotional hatred, that astounds me.'

D

In some ways, though, it is understandable. Visiting Americans don't have too much style. I remember a scene near the little town of Puerto Vallarda. Americans have built a luxury hotel here, about a mile along the shore from the old town with its squalor and campaniles. One afternoon I was sitting on the shore between the hotel and this town, doing some drawings of the jungle.

Occasional little groups of Americans, leaving the air-conditioned safety of their hotel, would set out to make the journey along the beach. But, at one point, it was crossed by a stretch of water that, although it looked shallow, was in fact deep.

Mexicans were able to cross it without any problem, tucking up their trousers or serapes to hip level. But not so the Gringos. It was a pathetic and poignant sight to see how party after party in their gay hats and raffia skirts would reach this stretch of water and then flounder, stagger, unable to contend with the strength of the current.

Meanwhile the water insidiously tore at their feet, gushingly, until at length one or two of the party would totally lose their balance and collapse and then, turning back, sodden, return to the safety of their air-conditioned hotel, with its palms and musak and artificially watered grass.

An attractive dark Irish-type woman wearing a gardenia in her hair, told me, 'I've got difficulties. I can't tell you. Difficulties. You don't know the least of them. That's why I can't go back to America. My husband has a big ranch in Texas. He is surrounded by men that are entirely narrow in their outlook. I can't stick them or him. Ours is one of the largest ranches in the whole of the States, and I'm sick of it.'

This woman, whenever she was introduced to a younger girl, would say, 'How attractive you are – I *hate* you. What lovely hair. What a shame. What lovely breasts. They're beautiful. You *disgust* me. You're so beautiful. I *hate* you.'

An American girl said to me, 'I'm a Career Guidance Adviser, in other words, a Vocationalist. People down here tend to be so all right that they don't need me. I came down here for a holiday. The people here are failures and they're all right. It's the successes back home that really need me. They need me bad.'

Mexico contains quite large numbers of American women living on alimony and men who live here so as to escape paying it. Some of the ex-marrieds are students, allegedly studying languages and living in boarding-houses, saying as they come down to breakfast, 'I don't know what went wrong with my homework last night. I got my genders wrong and my tenses all mixed up.'

Alimony must be paid to someone who is owed it in Mexico, but not necessarily *by* them. Thus there are many American men there to escape paying it.

There are a lot of hippies in Mexico, and also a few 'war heroes', too mixed up by service in American wars to be able to accept anything other than Mexican life any more.

One such man, standing in a bar of San Miguel de Allende, said, 'We're not hippies here. We're war veterans. For instance, see old Charlie over there. He's got more purple hearts (an award for valour) than he likes to mention. Another of us, see over there, Brian, he was a navigator. He saw dangerous action in many parts, and the result of this is that now he keeps on getting morse messages all the time, ticking through his brain. Endless morse messages. He can't stop them. The last one he got was about gonorrhoea. Sometimes the bomb goes off in his mind.

'All this should give you an idea of the class of people that come here.'

A Gringo actress told me, 'The Americans here are mocked. They are mocked by people with only a twentieth of their education. To be American in Mexico is to pass a tiny little boy and as you do so even he holds out his hand for pesos. The people here hate America. I don't hate America. America has done bad things but I happen to have been born there, and I don't hate it.'

A man told me, 'I'm going to write a newspaper article one day explaining to the American male how he can escape paying alimony. When I and my wife parted, alimony was set so fantastically high that I couldn't afford to live a decent life and pay it. So, I came down here where I don't have to pay any. I've got a new wife here and a child born on Mexican soil who is the legal owner of all my property although she's only twenty months old. We have a lot of fun here. More fun than I ever had before in my life.'

The Gringos I remember best of all are those who, getting together the equivalent of a few hundred pounds, come down to Mexico to spin their money out as long as they could. They would rent a palapa or jungle hut for two and six a week.

Often I heard them speak of the magic mushroom. One man,

an impressive former advertising executive, told me, 'I don't prize material possessions. I think such things are destructive. What I like to do is wander through the world as a citizen of the world, to be my own master. To write poetry, and to perform what Gregory Corso called "the act of sex with the creator".

'I think that most Americans here would agree that at some time of their life they have been caught in the urban horror, and felt that they were caught too long. At one time I thought that it was inadequacy in me that made me unable to conform to the office-block bureaucracy. It took me some time to realise that I was different in kind.

'I was in advertising. I was successful in advertising. But one day it came to seem to me that I was doing no more than gather the postage stamps of contemporary affluence, collecting the lucky tokens and cocoa tin lids of the O.K. society.

'I came to realise that my own contemporaries were caught in a terrible disaster. At weekends, as if leaving a devastated city, they would drive their motors through miles of traffic jams to what was once, long ago, decent country. I took a look around me. I would look at the people in the average train, and it would give me a pain in the heart. I came to feel that violence had been done to life in the streets of the great cities, violence to a country that was once beautiful. I came to feel that this was a mean people, living lost in the convolutions of their own repressions. I felt that they were saying, "Cut back that wanton immorally wantonning grass. Shave it. Prune these trees whose exuberance is too great and too violent. Fence in those tiring old ruins, they're too dangerous and far too romantic. Let them see who's boss, fence them around with eight foot high wire netting and pompous notices.

' "Then coat the sward with tarmac, and, lest man should ever wonder what he's lost, finish it off with a dash of synthetic sex." '

Many members of the great American drop-out are not responsible about property. On one occasion I heard one of the beats complaining, 'That's what Letitia does with your clothes. She goes off to Yelapa, the place that you can only get to by boat, and she spends a night there, and when she comes back, she says, "I took your clothes and I left them at Yelapa." What are you going to do then? Ask her *why* she took your clothes and left them at Yelapa? Ask her to go and get them back?'

Standing one night in a palapa I remember hearing a brash

cigar-smoking American say, helplessly, 'What are we all going to do then? Die? Is that what we ought to do? Is that the solution?'

In the room with us there were the American parents of a little girl who had come down here with them. She had died a week ago and I thought the man's remarks tactless.

But later, I learned that he had a liver complaint, and that he too, had come down here to die. Describing the reasons why he had given up a well-paid job and come to live down here, another drop-out said, 'They told me at the firm where I worked that I didn't dress smartly enough, I must do something about it. So I thought to myself, Well, I need the money, I'll conform to what they want of me and I went out and got an extremely smart suit and the following morning when I appeared in my suit, they complimented me on it, and said, "Well done. Excellent. We thought you'd see what we meant."

'But I was foolish enough to tell the man the real reason. I said, "Well, I didn't do it because I saw what you meant but just because I wanted the money, and so I thought I'd *better* do what you said." And he was so shocked at this that he sent me to the firm's psychiatrist and the psychiatrist said, "You must have a lot of worries", and I said I didn't have any worries. (I'd got someone else, another psychiatrist to help me figure, but I didn't tell him that.)

'So then he said, "Well, you seem very tense."

'So I said, "Well, wouldn't you be in all these new clothes?"

'And anyway, that's how I left my job, and came to Mexico.'

And I think to myself, These citizens of the American drop-out they're free, they accept you . . . if you go up to them in the street they accept you, they ask no questions like, Who are you? How old are you? Are you married? What's your name? What do you do for a living? They accept.

One of them said, scornfully, 'Modern civilised urban man! Say teenager to him, and he goes up to half cock. Say mini-skirt and he'll come prematurely.

Another story of drop-out concerned a girl of seventeen, long-haired and beautiful, who had made her way to rough terrain. There, passing by a lake, she stripped off her clothes and threw them into the water, keeping only an ornamental belt with a holster containing a sharp machete.

The girl lived wild like this for some time. Unfortunately, her parents had informed the police that she was missing, and one day rumours were heard about her being in the forest and some journalists came and were lucky enough to get a photograph of the lovely naked girl as she ran from them through the undergrowth.

There followed the combing of the jungle by police, the girl was captured, clothed, and taken back to her parents. She told reporters who visited her there that she was happy and glad that she'd been brought back to civilisation. But, soon after, she vanished again.

And I remember the words of another traveller to whom I spoke, 'I was travelling in the extreme Eastern area of the Yucatan and I heard the following story. That all tribes were mobilising for war through the entire area. Even Indians who had come down to the town were being called back to their camps in order to mobilise.'

'And what was the reason for the mobilisation?'

'Well, I was told that a beautiful girl was living in the forest, naked, making do for herself with the help of her long machete. The chiefs of the two rival tribes had fallen in love with her and each wanted her for his wife. So they were going to war. But she wanted neither of them.'

Was this the same girl? One day would more journalists go out into the jungle and find her here as well? And would the end of this be that once again some form of police force or perhaps the United States Navy itself would go out and bring her back to civilisation and her parents? And would she once more escape? If she did where would she end up this time?

12

Sands of La Ventosa

I am driving with two girls out on the road to Salina Cruz. In the darkness we pass a petrol station. Lorries are standing in this station and their drivers, many of them naked to the waist, are clustering round the petrol pumps, swapping cigarettes and buying mangos and tamales from children.

Up by the petrol pump a girl has the top of her blouse unbuttoned. Is this place by any chance also a brothel? There is an extraordinary feeling around. The warm heat of the tropical evening wafts over us. There is a feeling of darkness about this place which lies lost in the middle of the jungle.

Stopping by the road a little further on we find that the entire night has become full of a syncopated chorus of frogs, croaking amidst the bog, and a solitary cricket, and numerous curious birds, chirping amidst the trees.

The air is full of the silent brightness of lightning, and of those brightnesses – the brightness of fire-flies and of falling stars. And now in the fly-blown city of Salina Cruz, we eat fish foods in a huge concrete room rather like a restaurant at the English seaside.

I have heard that you can sleep in hammocks on the beach of a place called La Ventosa, and, as the night is hot, we decide to go there. We drive down the wide streets of this once important port, streets that now appear to have been sifted over with sand, so that the sound of the car wheels on the sand makes a soft crunching sound. We ask directions from a man. He says, 'It's quite easy, turn left and left again. Then left again, right, and left once more.'

We continue, bumping over the unmade roads between the houses, trying to follow his directions. At one point no less than three different lefts present themselves. Which one should we take?

'We'd better go back and ask the man again.'

But we get lost on the way back and find ourselves in a street that has got totally overwhelmed with sand, completely blocked.

Large numbers of people are drinking in a big shed built across the road, its top consisting of a roof made of pine branches. I approach one of the least drunk groups and ask the way to La Ventosa. The result is electrifying. People spring to their feet, thrust me down on to the chair, bombard me with statements about La Ventosa, shaking their heads, placing hands round their necks in a strangling position.

'It is not safe to go there. There are many Ladrones on the way. Many robbers. Murderers. Bad men. A very bad place to go.'

Another man makes a gesture as of somebody turning a knife in my ribs. Another man adopts a more crafty attitude to me, 'But I can accompany you there if you would like.'

Another man shouts, 'Psst. Don't go with him, he is a Ladrone. No good. No good to you. A very bad man.' He puts his two fingers one to each side of his nose, in a sinister gesture, drawing them up tight round his nostrils. Perhaps another gesture indicating suffo-cation.

One of the group, suddenly turns on me. 'You are Spanish,' he shouts.

Again the whole group act as though they had been electrified, look at me angrily. It is some time before I am able to establish that I am not Spanish. Unaccountably I forget the Spanish words for 'no' and 'yes'. I am beginning to realise how drunk they all are. They are asking the girls to dance, keep putting their hands on the girls' shoulders, thrusting new bottles of wine and beer into our hands, tilting them towards our mouths, forcing us to drink. A man comes over from another table and says to one of the girls, 'Leave all this beer, I will give you tequila if you come to my table.'

'Don't go with him. Don't go with him.'

Why this consternation that we are going to La Ventosa?

I say to the girls, 'I think we ought to go. I don't like the atmosphere here. When I say 'go', jump to your feet and make for the car as fast as you can.'

The girls don't really seem to understand what's going on, partly because they don't understand Spanish as well as I do. When I say 'go' there is not the burst of electrifying action that I had hoped for. The girls get up and hobble incompetently towards the car. And the drunken crowd from the bar are staggering after us, as we jump into the car they cluster round it, the car stalls, it won't go, and still people are offering to take us to La Ventosa, saying, 'Yes, you'll be quite safe there,' while others insist that we mustn't go. 'There are so many bad men there. Ladrones, robbers!'

It is only later that I learn what really was going on here. It seems that, a few weeks before, a girl, like us, asked the way to La Ventosa. She was seen talking to the police. The next thing that was heard of her was when she was found dead on the beach. It was against whatever unknown death befell her that the men were offering to protect us.

There is a place not far from here called Tehuantepec, where society has become woman-dominated. The men, shabby creatures, stay back home to look after the children, wear old jeans and battered shoes, and sit around the square all day playing dominoes. The women, on the other hand, are beautiful. They dress splendidly in bright coloured silks, great dresses with huge exotic bustles and magnificent headgear. They seem like wonderful peacocks as they sweep about, and they despise men. One of their tricks is to pose for a Gringo man against an exotic background of palms or whatever, and then, when he tries to photograph them, run away, shrieking with laughter.

I wander through the market, noticing women of great beauty with long raven locks falling down their backs, wearing black velvet blouses picked out with flowers, and long flowing cotton skirts with bright colours down to their feet.

Now I am in the fruit market, and there are fantastic women striding by with baskets of avocado pears on their heads, baskets of green bananas, the fruit they call crush, great piles of coconuts. I go up to a counter and a woman in an orange velvet blouse and bright green skirt sprinkled with pink roses and a pink scarf round her head hacks a hole in the top for me to drink the green pungent liquid, and then she shatters it across with a violent blow from her machete, so that I can eat the white inner soft shell. Further into the market I notice a brilliant green parrot sitting on the side of a basket. The roof is stitched from numerous pieces of linen sheet and pink perspex and supported on the twisted shapes of trees. There are very few men around. The place is stuffed with women, proud, forthright, overbearing and amazingly beautiful.

Often they sit or lounge in positions of total abandonment with their feet up on the sides of the booths, legs wide apart, the sort of positions usually only used by men. One of the less active of the few men present is one who owns a booth that is selling pots. Apparently overwhelmed by these luxuriant striding women, he has hung a hammock across the booth and is sleeping quietly.

Outside, I stand and watch buses put in from the outlying provinces, filled with women. Most of the women's hair is plaited in brilliant red or other coloured braid. Another bus goes past with its roof piled high with small pink, yellow and green plastic ornamental cushions.

The place has a quality of style quite different from any of the male-dominated markets I've been to, their shabbiness, their squalor. Now I am travelling by train. In the darkness I pass little farms, outside which are tables lit with oil-lamps round which families sit. Now in the night we stop at a station larger than the others and the corridors are completely filled with merchandise of every sort, pots, baskets of eggs, everything conceivable.

People have got lighted lanterns with them, they climb down from the train onto the platform where their families are camped awaiting them. The entire platform is a sea of dark faces and the shapes of their white hats across which the light flashes, and the guard urging them to hurry. The ringing of a bell. The corridors of the train twist as we continue through the mountains. I wish I could see the way we're going. The passengers lie huddled together. There is a grace about these people that I haven't found in the British. Nature has been kinder to them, perhaps, than to some of the denizens of the remote and misty lands of Albion. The light is dim in the third-class carriages and all along the sides are cardboard boxes tied with string, hanging down from the racks, swaying as we go.

Now it is morning. At the end of each compartment there are steps leading out into the open air. People are standing on these steps, sniffing the morning air. The carriages of the railway here have written on them 'N de M'.

13

Magic Mountain

The volcanic mountain of Popocatepetl is a symbol for Mexico, with its sister mountain, Ixtacchihuatl. A mountain climbing professor was introduced to me who promised that he would take me to the top. 'Tomorrow – tomorrow,' he exclaimed. 'Tomorrow at seven-thirty I will call at your hotel.'

Tomorrow dawned and there was no professor. The same thing happened the following day, and the following day again, and for a while my days assumed a similar pattern – I would go to bed early, dossing down in expectancy, only to wake up some time around eight or eight-thirty in the realisation that, once more, the professor hadn't come. This went on for five days until, unable to bear this waiting any longer, I decided to set out on my own.

When I had finally located the station I found it to be an imposing brick edifice, at the foot of whose arches large numbers of families were camped, families lying beneath blankets under the old-fashioned porticos, families sitting on the steps that lead up to the station, families assembled beneath the lofty brick arches.

A girl called Amatista approached me. She handed me a card which said, 'Orientation. By Amatista.'

I bought a ticket and boarded the narrow train and soon we were running out of town. Like small mountain ranges, there were the sudden graves of autos, vast piled up skeletons of motors on the desert-like land, emerging behind the wide expanse of shack-like houses.

Farther out into the country, I noticed a single narrow little house standing in the midst of its space of land, with a Cadillac bonnet firmly sitting on its roof. And now the last of the little concrete shacks was past us.

The train was tiny, uncomfortable, with wooden seats. The

engine somewhere far ahead was hooting constantly. The floor
and walls of the carriage were patchily painted in a pretty shade
of light blue. There was also an exotically painted Pepsi-cola sign.

The carriage was full of dust now, hanging over the seats and
passengers, choking. I stood up and looked out of the window and
saw again more dust, great clouds of dust sweeping across the arid
countryside, and, far ahead through clouds of dust, the mountains
reaching up into the sky, ringed with clouds. The stations at which
we stopped every now and again seemed to have no names, nor
indication that they were stations. Rather, they were just little
booths standing by the track. One of them was beautiful, like a
rose-covered bower, roses everywhere. From amongst these roses a
man with a big basket filled with various sorts of melons joined us.

Now the train had at last left the plain and was climbing up into
the mountains. And at length, after some hours of hooting and
wandering, it put us down in the town of Amecameca, a pretty
little town with palm trees, and a few sparse examples of Spanish
Colonial architecture. In the middle of the square was a fountain
with a basin, at the moment dry, filled with rubbish.

I went into a bar and drank sweet milk-like pulque, and bought
two cakes and a couple of bars of chocolate. A man approached
me, and, guessing my intentions, offered to take me up the first
stage of the mountain. He produced a pencil stub and drew out a
winding route on the back of a cigarette packet, putting his hands
in the form of prayer to indicate the top of the mountain. Then
underneath he wrote in large caterpillar-like capitals the provisions
that he felt we would need – Naranja – Azucar – Cafe – Tequila –
oranges, sugar, coffee, tequila. But I didn't want company. If I had,
I would have waited for the professor. I left the pulqueria.

'Then there is tequila,' he cried after me, coming to the door
with its beaded curtain. 'It helps you to see the view – and views
you would never see when you are sober!'

I crossed a railway track and began to climb up long steps
which wound up to a sanctuary at the top of a hill. Staggering up
these long steps, regretting that I had drunk so much pulque,
turning occasionally to watch the great dust clouds swirl up the
valley behind, as I made my way up the endless steps, past the
various stations of the cross, I passed a man crawling up on his
bloody knees, looking round at me nervously as if he thought that
I might hit him, then continuing his slow solitary painful creep up

the hill. Now three women were coming towards me down the long path that leads from the sanctuary. They were singing some baleful old-fashioned chant – *Que vida de descanso para el aue huye del ruido mundano* – and behind them there was a boy limping along, one leg longer than the other. Perhaps they'd come to try to get a cure for this cripple. So concerned were they with their singing that they didn't notice at one point, where the steps turned sharply, that they had left the path altogether. They went on, still singing, wandering off into the undergrowth, the boy limping gamely behind them. I sat down and watched them for a moment, for it was very hot.

A few minutes later and the same sound of chanting was heard and the same group of heavily shawled women re-emerged still singing, from the undergrowth, apparently unabashed by their mistake, the boy still plodding behind them. They continued their walk ahead of me.

Looking downhill, I saw a priest approaching, leading a crowd of forty women, and this time not on their knees. At each station of the cross they stopped to have a lecture and a brief prayer, followed by a spontaneous chant. Behind them as they trailed up the hill came two men bearing trays of glutinous looking rock in pink and purple. I followed them to the top, where they settled down outside the church in the shade of the big porch, listening to the service that was coming from inside. Directly the last Amen was past, there was a great scramble to unpack food from a series of baskets and cloths. And so they dined among the graves on the food that they had brought with them, beneath a notice above a decrepit door that said, SACRISTIA, and another notice in similar angular capitals over a second door that said, REFRESCOS.

Leaving the flock of women clustered round the gravestones, I went into the church and sat down, glad to get out of the heat. In front of me, beneath a vast dome, was a sort of old-fashioned cave which had got the head of Christ in it and two large strong boxes labelled, DEPOSITE A QUI SU LIMOSNA Y QUE DIOS LE BENDIGA – Put your offerings here in order that God may bless you. I continued up the hill behind the sanctuary in the gruelling heat until I reached yet another sanctuary, a church sitting on the very top of this little hill, and more decrepit than the other. There was plaster flaking from the walls, large cracks across the front, and the whole church was held together with great wires that looked as if they went completely round it. The church had tall wooden panelled doors, one of which seemed to be stuck permanently open. There were only two pews inside. The floor seemed somewhat mouldy, and at its further end amidst all this decrepitude there was an altar covered with bowls of flowers.

Outside, amongst the population of gravestones, there stood an old fountain with a sculptured bowl. There was no water in it, only a pig poking up his nose from somewhere inside the dry fountain, snorting, hiding in the hot shadow of some planks that had been placed across the top to keep the sun off him. Round the back of the church there was an old house made of sleepers and corrugated iron. The whole mountain seemed to shake as far beneath us the train ran by on its tracks, set in the spongy mud of the valley.

Now I was lurching along a dusty road in an ancient car through the golden evening light, past the strange green depths of trees. The car, stuffed with people, jolted along a rutty road, till we reached a sort of triumphal arch made of wilted green boughs, and emerged amongst old stone houses and a Spanish style church.

Sitting beside me in the motor, an old man in faded jeans and a white shirt was speaking to me earnestly. I couldn't understand what he was saying. Probably he was warning me not to be rooked by the taxi driver.

We jerked past a little collection of mud-brick hovels, with men standing at the doors. The road got steeper and behind us in the valley the sun was setting. We were amongst trees, there was a chain across the road and we had to rouse an old man to loose it for us and let us through. Now it was dark and there was only the white moon in front, shining at us suddenly white and brilliant like the headlamp of a car.

We reached what I took to be the end of the road. I paid the driver and wandered off through the dark, munching one of the twelve oranges that I bought in town, wondering whether by the time I got to the top of the mountain I would be wishing that I had kept it. And I noticed that I was still on a road of sorts. The man had put me down short.

As I walked on upwards amongst the pine trees, of a sudden there emerged the huge whitey-blue summit of Popocatepetl with snow streaming down over its rocks as if it had been poured. It was all dead quiet now in the moonlight, all I could hear was my own breathing. Already I was at thirteen or fourteen thousand feet. I continued, and after an hour reached a vantage point from which the mountain looked like slightly melting white ice. A quiet dog came stealthily up to me from out of the trees and sat watching me, waiting. I supposed he lived wild, and that his subsistence was from food given him by visitors who had come this far to sit and gaze at the mountain.

I spent a cold night under my blanket, beside a spring at the beginning of the grey volcanic shale. The next morning a brilliant orange sun was shining at me earnestly as I set forth to attempt the ascent of the mountain. I knew that I must start early, otherwise I would not be back by sundown. There were dust clouds all around me, dust clouds shooting up in dense swarms from the volcanic shale, and the occasional blast of cold air swinging down from the summit. I was staggering forward through the hard grey ashes of the volcanic shale, the whole mountain seemed to be made of it. There were muddy tongues of snow now reaching down beside the track, hollowed along the side by runnels of water like the sides of slag heaps.

It was spongy, awkward going. Whirlwinds whisked the dust up into the air and it circled with a dark gritty hissing sound over my head. It was painful, too. It grazed my skin as it blew past me, drifting almost as if it were performing a slow dance over the empty, black, steep, downward curves of the hill in the wind that came up from the valley. The peaks ahead, hidden beneath the snow, glittered white amid the grey black shale. And now there was the noise all around me of water – water thrusting itself out from under the ice whose grey dirty tongues stretched down towards me.

I saw just above me a sobering sight – a sinister collection of crosses standing on a jutting outcrop of the mountain, made of wrought iron. Panting, I climbed closer. One cross was ornate, with plastic flowers wired to it and also an ice-pick which must have belonged to the person whose death it commemorated. There was a photograph on porcelain in its centre of a young boy. One of the crosses had holes in it and the wind hooted through these holes in a dreary manner. I looked back now past the crosses, and saw, far below me, long lines of mist streaking slowly across the valley. All around this cross there stood the jumbled glittering shapes of rocks, scattered where they had fallen.

Overhead I heard the croak of a large black crow and looked up to see him watching me sinisterly. Apart from the rushing water and the softly hooting cross, and the sound of the crow, the only other sound was the occasional clatter of snow as it detached itself from the rest of the glacier and went slithering down the grey dust of the mountain.

And now things were beginning to get hard for me. The air was very thin here and I realised that I must have beaten my previous record – I must be higher than the thirteen thousand five hundred feet which was my previous record when I climbed the mountain of Ras Degien in Ethiopia. The air was so thin that I was panting all the time now. Humiliatingly, I couldn't get into my lungs enough breath to keep me going. And I was frightened now. I felt I couldn't go on any more. Even though I hadn't even reached the snow belt yet, I was frightened and exhausted. Frightened of avalanches, and short of air.

There was a precipitous face of rock that stuck out from the side of the mountain, one precarious piece of horizontal in a land-scape that was as steep otherwise as the side of a roof. I lay down here and slept. The sun hurtled down with all his force on my face, and all I felt was a blissful peace that my aching limbs were for the moment at rest.

When I awoke, a strange thing happened. My tiredness seemed to have gone and all that I was conscious of now was an over-powering urge to get to the top of the mountain if I possibly could. I didn't think about it any more. Instead I found myself once more struggling upwards, up the side of the mountain. Now I had reached the edge of the snow, and a new problem presented itself. For, as I stepped up onto the glittering surface of the snow, I realised that I could not go any further. My shoes slipped back-wards as fast as I stepped forward, in a moment I was flat on my bottom, sliding back down the snow ignominiously to the point where it gave way to volcanic shale again. This happened five times.

And then something occurred which was quite astounding. Because, there at my feet where the shale petered out and gave way to snow, I saw a couple of contraptions made of iron that I immediately realised must be ice shoes. There were six rusty spikes on each, and, round their top, leather thongs and buckles. They were designed to clamp on over shoes. I clamped them over my shoes and once more stepped up onto the snow. And, thus equipped, I was able slowly, stamping sharp holes in the snow as I went, to continue my ascent of the mountain. Even so, the going wasn't easy. I was panting all the time now and my mouth felt dry as old leather.

Twelve steps, I told myself, and then stop and count twenty, then twelve steps, perhaps you can stretch it to fourteen steps, then stop, count twenty again. I could feel my heart beating harder and harder all the time as I stepped forward. As I reached the twelfth step the pounding inside my rib cage was almost intolerable. None the less, after I had rested, I continued my self-ordained ordeal. Now madness had gripped me. Far below now, looking back, I could see the distant place where I had eaten all but one of my oranges the night before, and had given a scrap to the dog. Now that place seemed minute and very peaceful compared to the horror of this hillside. My eyes were hurting from the glare of the snow and I noticed that the snow was beginning to be ridged into vast waves, whose surface was ice. As I dislodged pieces of this snow or ice they began to cascade down the mountain with a sinister, dry, glittering quality of sound like a skeleton's bones rattling.

I continued to stagger on upwards. The snow became even stranger here, broken into huge frozen hillocks or mountains with crevasses in between them four or five feet deep. Each step now was a pain, a deliberation. I find it hard to describe now the extraordinary will power that was necessary just to keep putting one foot in front of the other, that situation of standing dizzy on a steep slope, as steep as the roof of a house, and willing myself not to lie down but to continue, to put one foot in front of the other.

There was a dizzying blinding flash of snow in my eyes all the time, and every now and again I rolled stones down behind me to see how much danger there might be of avalanches falling on me and burying me.

I remember lying in the sun at intervals feeling safe and sick, then looking downwards, down the hill, with a turning over of my heart and a reeling sensation at the steep abandon of the creamy slope as it stretched down underneath me, and always high above me the heartless sun.

Now I was no longer taking twelve steps and resting while I counted eighteen, not even taking twelve steps and resting for twenty-four. I was resting for twenty-four and then taking five steps.

The frozen waves now were really mountainous, they were three feet high, each time I felt as if I would never be able to cross them. And I was floundering, clambering, quite unable to control my movements, and the tall waves of snow seemed like the waves of the sea, rampant, seeming to be plotting to baffle and destroy me.

Insensate, not really noticing what I was doing, as I was clambering over yet one more wave, I saw all of a sudden with horror that there were no more waves beyond, that the tall ascending waves of the icy snow had given way to something different, the yielding descending shale edge of a circular pit, sudden, vast, deep. One step more, one heedless movement, would have taken me over the edge. I drew back, clinging on for life and safety, and saw below me the vast crater of the mountain stretching down inside thousands of feet.

Now I was sitting on the knife edge of the crater, and I could see an oily yellow mist rising nastily up towards me from the lava. Next, looking up once again with my painful eyes to the rim, I noticed that the walls of this mighty crater were like the walls of a cathedral, so twisted and pitted were they with organ pipe convolutions of stalactites and I knew that I ought to be going down, and yet it was so extraordinary and wonderful here – I listened for a moment, hearing the sounds of the occasional stone plopping its lonely desolate path down the empty thousands of feet of the ravine. The old rocks here were coloured green and red. There were jagged edges of ice-like teeth all round the top of the crater like castellations, and I was leaning back all the time, because there seemed no reason why the shale on which I sat should not slip headlong over the edge into the crater, and it seemed safer leaning back. I was writing down frenzied notes in my notebook, looking up at the sun to judge how long I had. I must go. Yet I was hypnotised by it, wanting to stay here years and write everything I saw and always the sun was slanting down, lighting the further side of the crater with a brilliant blaze, and now as I waited the crater was already caught in a spiral of darkness and always there was that terrible seething searing smoke coming up from the bottom, and, not loosened by me, there was still far below the dry sound of stones falling their lonely way down into the depths of the ravine. And I thought to myself – if you fell down there there would be no rescue.

The rocks of the crater seemed immemorably old, like the walls of ancient cathedrals ribbed and corrugated in a succession of pinnacles and bastions. And the snow round its top had dots of black shale caught in it like currants in cream.

Now I allowed myself the luxury of my last orange. I had been looking forward to this orange for the last few hours, keeping it for the time when my mouth would be so dry that I felt I couldn't go on any longer. This time had now come. Oh, that parched numb dryness! I got the orange out from my pocket and bit into it hungrily. But – horror! The inside of the orange was nothing but total corruption, a complete crawling mass of worms.

And so I started off back down the mountain, and on the way down I remember being too exhausted even to step any more, but sitting down on my behind and sliding down the snow-covered slopes. And I found I couldn't stop – there was the fresh terror of getting out of control and sliding too far, the searing pain of my bottom dragging along the snow.

In a remarkably short time I was getting to the end of the snow and stumbling, drifting, staggering down through the shale in the semi-darkness on my bottom. I fell, slid, rolled, and thought, Careful, don't break your leg. The sun was off the slope now. And now, the first trickle of melted water. I could have a drink. I filled my hands with it and drank. A lovely muddy brackish taste. And saw how the melted water and lava had coiled into beautiful shapes at the bottom of the flowing water.

The sun had left a white line behind me at the highest point of the peak. My boots were full of shale as I continued down, past those sinister crosses.

It had been dark some while and I had staggered more miles when, suddenly through the darkness, I could see the glimmering windows of a mountain hut. Peering through the window I saw oil lamps on the long tables, and there were many people inside, a fire blazing in a vast stone hearth, and the scene was lit with innumerable candles.

When I made myself known a man invited me in, pointing out vast bottles filled with pulque, and bottles containing two different types of rum. There was his sister, his wife, his wife's three sisters, and, scattered around the room already fast asleep, innumerable little children. And they were singing a succession of old songs.

The man said to me, 'My daughter is unmarried, she would do for you.'

A young boy sang what he called American songs – strange tuneless ditties on one note, which he must have picked up from a juke-box. After each one that he sang, he asked, 'Le gusta?' 'Do you like it?' And I lied, 'Yes.' At length, drunk with tequila, in turn all of them sank to rest on the floor, and I did too, and the fire, stoked before we slept, slowly died down through the night.

The following morning there were countless little babies and children swarming everywhere, and one girl lying ill amid the piles of gaudy filthy blankets, breathing deeply.

Out through the window the whole mountain seemed to steam this morning. Looking back at the slopes of Popocatepetl, I saw them obscured in the blinding dust and steam that was coming down from the volcano. The winds had got up, it was wild today, the top of Popo was hardly visible. Not good to climb today.

The women were tying up their belongings in cardboard boxes, and stacking mattresses in the back of the lorry. The men were eating steak for their breakfast, cooked on the same fire that kept us warm during the night. And I saw a prayer written up on the wall, NUESTRA SEÑORA DE LAS MONTAÑAS, RUEGUE POR NOSOTROS.

Through the window I saw parked a small green lorry labelled *Servicio particular. Commerciante en general.* Everyone packed into the lorry, and the little children came up to me and gave me oranges as they said goodbye. And I asked if I might stay alone in the hut there through the day in front of the hanging mists of Popocatepetl.

Later, one day, I was wandering through a poor part of Mexico City, through the bright pink and green little municipal houses, where the streets have no names, only numbers like Oriente 71014 or 27247, wandering through the endless one-storey housing estate which seems to stretch on and on for ever through hundreds of thousands of houses, passing little shrines where chunks of old motor cars were hanging up along streets thronged with people. Suddenly a tiny girl in a bright yellow muslin frock, very beautiful, accosted me. 'Por aqui! Por aqui!' 'This way! This way!' I followed her, wondering what on earth she could want, wondering whether she was leading me to a brothel. I entered the narrow doorway which she showed me and found myself in a courtyard surrounded by six one-roomed houses again absolutely filled with people. And then I recognised that by some astounding chance fate had led me to the one street in the whole of Mexico City's population of seven million, where they lived. Their house was in a tiny room whose doors and windows were covered with fleecy-covered transparent muslin, yellow and pink. There was one bed in the middle covered with numerous gaudy beautiful counterpanes on which a little baby was sleeping. The unmarried daughter that he had thought might do for me sat also on the bed, gazing at me in a mournful manner.

And so we sat contented, in this courtyard which contained five other little one-roomed houses and an infinite amount of gaudy washing, telling each other stories, singing.

14

Acapulco

I am in a bus travelling down to Acapulco and, looking out through its windows into the evening, think that there are times when I despair of describing this country, it is so beautiful. We are travelling through a lyrical, fantastic, empty countryside, ribbed with villages, enriched with small yet graceful trees that cast long shadows on all the grassy slopes on which they stand.

A girl, a baby tied to her back with a shawl, is leading two other children by the hand. She walks over this illimitable countryside of rock, trees and pastures which have never been partitioned. Far below in the valley I see the blue and white campanile of a church that the Spanish must have built here.

We arrive late that night in Taxco, and are at once surrounded by little boys rushing up saying, 'What do you want? What do you want?' People offering everything from very cheap bits of silver, to old leather, to a cheap hotel.

We are stumbling up the very steep cobbled paths. At length we reach a small square, and I look round in vain for the hotel that we have been recommended – the Hotel Jardin. The cathedral stretches above us, with the fantastic Rococo multiplicity of its pink windows and pillars. I can see no sign of the hotel and at length ask a man who is sitting with his family by the foot of a building next door. 'Well, of course, this is it,' he exclaims. And now I notice a small wooden sign above his head that says, 'Hotel'.

He leads me upstairs and shows me a nice room with a U-shaped balcony, which allows a view across to the mountains amongst which this town stands. 'Yes, we'll have this.' We go downstairs again and I am signing the register when the man's plans seems to change, for he suddenly anounces, 'This is not the room for you.'

Again we go up the stairs and he demonstrates another room,

even nicer than the previous one. Once more we go down and pay, and again he changes his mind, and shows us an even nicer room. Here I lie, hearing the soft sounds of evening floating up from outside.

The mountains beside the road become even more chaotic, crumpled together, forced towards the sky as if at the whim of some heedless yet powerful hand. Among the mountains the countryside is littered with vast round white boulders as big as houses, and amidst these a broad white river runs between sandbanks of red earth. There are palm trees waving here, waving their strange green-white arms in profusion, standing amidst the boulders. Now the bus I am in, the Estrella del Oro, passes the first straggling outposts of Acapulco, a collection of shacks that emerge from among the undergrowth. Amongst the boulders are little houses made of corrugated iron and oiled paper, bits of bamboo, old bits of wood, anything that can be pressed into service. The atmosphere of these terraced, totally decrepit, brightly painted little houses amongst which hangs washing, seems idyllic. We pass a market, a sea of rickety counters under tatty sheds of corrugated iron, and there is brightly coloured washing hanging, washing everywhere. And people go about their business slowly, deliberately, we're in the tropics now and when we leave the air-conditioned bus I know that the stench and waft of the heat will hit us in all its fury and we will begin to sweat. And now the number of little cabins and cantinas is multiplying amongst the boulders, there are no roads to these little residences, only red dirt tracks. There is a shrine, with a life-sized Christ hanging from it surrounded by pink and white plastic roses and now a level space on which stands a basket-ball pitch, with, planted on top of one of the goals, a vast Coca-cola bottle, one and a half times the size of a man.

Beyond is the wide blue sweep of the waters, the glory of the luxury hotels standing up along them, and soon now the bus will be running along the shore behind these same hotels, close to where those blue-green waters lap placidly against the tourists who sit beneath the little thatched roofs on wooden chairs and sip through straws from green coconuts filled with rum.

There are various American-owned eating places along this esplanade, Big-boy, Dennys, Sanbournes, where you can get food and drink so cold that it freezes you, and hamburgers and other similar rubbish to fill you up.

The Condesa is the smartest beach, and is the parade ground for the poufs of the town. Here comes a dusky almost negroid Mexican, and he walks along in the style of, 'Well here I am just strolling along'. A North American pouf walks past, set well back on his haunches, holding a cocktail glass; he has peroxide blond hair.

The beach is empty today. The story is that some Gringo boys and girls were making love on the beach and smoking pot and the police came and took them away. So people are wary. As I am swimming an arm parts the water. The owner of the arm emerges from beneath the waters, all dripping, holding a cross. It is a salesman. He wants to sell me 'sacred American crosses'.

Mexican people, as I have met them, are capable of smiling even as they are planning to rob you or worse, and this perhaps is bad. But they are none of them capable of that intensity of hatred that even the simplest British shopkeeper seems able, on occasion, to project towards his customers. They are less sick perhaps than we are.

A large lorry goes by labelled TRANSPORTO SANITARIO DE CARNES and in the cabin a lovely Mexican girl sits on the driver's lap. Our bus, lemon-green in colour and with seats so close together that it is only possible for me to sit on one by putting my knees out sideways beside me, lurches through and into a series of pot-holes with a number of bangs and crashes as we go up the hillside above Acapulco to a little colony of chalets called Las Brisas.

If you stay there you get a pink and white striped jeep thrown in along with your chalet. Beyond that, where the road passes the water-shed, now you can see the view and the driver has been grinding into his gears in a rather scarey manner, now the engine of the bus stops and although he tries to jump it into gear, all the bus does is shudder and give out a strange animal whimper. At length the driver gives up, and, planting his feet firmly on the brake, he leans over his wheel and appears to fall asleep.

People get out from the bus and begin to walk down the long hill towards the distant line of breakers. Others decide to stay in the bus and wait till the next one comes. Everyone is just settling down when the bus gives a lurch and starts to cruise once more down the hill. People spring to their feet and shout in terror. The driver, who had fallen asleep, wakes up and hastily slams his foot back on the brake.

As we sit on the beach there pass an endless succession of sales-men. A man whose waist is loaded with spectacles. Two young men trying to persuade me to do scuba diving, or as the young man calls it scuba-duba. He guesses the ages of girls he tries to sell scuba-duba to. 'How did you learn to guess?' 'I learn in bed. I not able to tell if they have clothes on.'

We go to the empty endless splendour of the Acapulco Hilton, with immensely tall windows lining the public rooms, but which do not give onto the air, only onto concrete. Some conversation is going on there, and, hung up in drooping, gaudy, red letters are the names of a firm – SEXON – and underneath, in smaller letters, 'The Fun Company'. Another smaller notice, indicating the position of some exhibit or other, says *Publicidad,* (Publicity, Dad). And now a bearded man passes by, offering to draw my portrait.

The hotel seems vast and empty, at one point there's a complete shopping arcade, built to look like a ship. Parties of beautifully dressed Americans are wandering back and forth from one end of the hotel to the other through these vast, empty, air-conditioned chambers, in search of joy. We have a drink near the lifts, in a bar which gives onto a view of a long vista of concrete arches, lined by brass electric lamps, lit with an authentic Mexican stained-glass window. A glass of beer costs me ten shillings. Nearby are the central lifts of the hotel, and couples of beautifully dressed Americans are constantly entering and emerging from the lifts. Their feet are bare – naked feet are in order in the Acapulco Hilton. Across these spotless marble floors the tender feet of the North Americans come to no harm.

Later we go out on the beach and sit in a thatched hut con-taining a tractor (used for raking the beach) while the thunder flashingly lights up the beautiful stretches of the bay. Momentarily from the darkness a little island appears with the false colours of a picture postcard. And where we sit, suddenly a vast river starts surging past, lit up in the lightning flashes, a vast tongue of dirty swirling water surging across the beach, filled with all types of debris, coconut husks.

Near the Mirador Hotel, from whose balconies divers make their precipitous dive of ninety-two feet into the water far below, there stands the thirty-foot high statue of a Gringo girl in a bathing-dress, advertising some airline. Not far away there is a tent, and beside it a large notice saying, *Secretaria del Patrimonio Nationale*.

People sell every imaginable type of merchandise, as you sit in chairs beneath little thatched roofs by the sea. A man comes round offering to paint my picture, and another is selling coconut husks filled with rum. One sells coral necklaces. Another, pots of brilliant green ice-cream.

By the shore, Mexicans are taking their dug-out canoes out into the water to fish. And, from these same depths, emerge a shoal of scuba-divers complete with instructor – bulky and soundly constructed American girls mainly, onto whose lumpy bodies the lovely Mexican boys tie the paraphernalia of huge belts, oxygen cylinders, machetes, masks.

A young Mexican man and his girl sit on the shore, watching a Gringo man and his girl rolling, playing in the exotic surf. When they go back on the shore they try to do it themselves. But they can't. They are locked in their own inhibitions, tragically tied. Just for a moment they begin to be happy and have fun, then the girl returns and sits alone on a rock, and the man is left to his mournful swimming on his own.

A man passes by with a wheelbarrow containing various bottles of liquor. I read from the brochure of a moonlight cruise in which the captions have got in the wrong places. A picture of a donkey being fed from a bottle of beer while a pirate complete with eye-patch, cutlass, brass boots and striped red trousers watches admiringly, is captioned, 'A delicious buffet is served. Beer and refreshments.'

In another picture this same pirate, but with his cutlass this time in his mouth, is seen attempting to strangle a beautiful blonde, while her boyfriend looks on ineffectually. This is captioned, 'Admire the most beautiful scenery and the sunset.'

A third picture, showing a girl perched on the railings in front of a lifeboat while the inimitable blue sea stretches away behind her is labelled, 'Joy and atmosphere with two dance areas.'

And a final photograph of two people dancing cheek to cheek in a bar is labelled merely, 'Delicious snacks. A comfortable seat for each person.'

Saturday night in Acapulco – the air is vibrant with the screech-ing sirens of police cars and very rare scattered bursts of what sounds like gunfire and the constant howling of dogs. The wide famous bay stretches out below my hotel window now in the warm darkness, lit by all its innumerable coloured lights, brilliantly twinkling in these closer areas where the luxury hotels are, sporadic and tawdry in those further hill areas where the Mexican workers have their shacks.

In the air-conditioned gloom of the luxury hotels lining the coast the Gringo guests dance to smoochy music, and around the central square the neon-lit cafés are filled with Mexicans, and there are cars cruising in and around the zoccalo filled with men. The town tonight is filled with sailors from one of the French ships in port. The cafés here serve milk shakes, lager-type beer, ice cream, coffee, and steak if you want it.

There is a family of the poorer type of Mexican here, from the ill-favoured little shanty-towns that climb up the hills behind Acapulco, often without proper roads. From there they have a first-rate view of the town and the gorgeous bay and all that luxury stretched out below them, and the wind blows cooler on them up there in their shacks. And the man says, as he settles in the women at the café, 'Ah, yes, waiter, good evening, waiter,' imitating the visiting Gringos.

And in a fashionable discotheque, there is a psychedelic light-show like any other, the lights flashing on bright, then complete darkness so that you seem to be in a silent movie, and the rich Mexicans and the rich Gringos (those who can afford the fifteen peso entry fee), are showing off their latest clothes bought at the smart American shops, and, as one of them says, 'It's so necessary to have a smart place, so necessary that it should be the smartest, that they can't admit that it stinks. . . .'

My girl says to me, holding my hand, 'This town does have a smell, it is like plastic buttons when you iron them.' Along the streets now the policemen begin their night-time walk. They blow whistles as they go, quiet and melodious whistles soft like a bird's song punctuating the night with their soft plaintive little statements.

And in the boats that bob beside the quay, amongst them the GLASS BOTTOM BOAT (BARCA CON FONDO DE CRISTAL), people are sleeping. No need really for beds in this heat, the raggedy figures snore in the expensive chairs designed for the hirers of the boats.

And in this part of town it is quiet, but over in the brothel section there is life still going on. Over there, inland, where the streets are still not paved, are the dance-halls which cater for the visiting sailors, and a few rather drunk looking Gringos and anyone who can rake a few pesos together.

We turn off the concrete highway and the car lurches along a craggy surface of rutted mud. Dust rises thickly into the hot air, there are quite a number of taxis nosing their way along the road towards the various houses of pleasure, and the headlights light up the bare shoulders and white shirts of men trudging on amidst this same heavy faintly luminous dusk.

The car lurches up into a wide entrance and we are in a large circular enclosure, just about an acre in all. Round the outside are the pleasant little houses of the prostitutes and in the middle a coloured fountain falling down in three layers and a huge thatched hut whose lofty spires contain revolving air fans. The floodlit tropical vegetation, palms, coconuts, hanging bananas are lit and the purple and yellow is so amazing that people born into cold climates might think that they were artificial, so luxuriant and wonderful are they.

Music is belting out from here in a great din, the usual mariachi thrum thrum and now we get inside the huge palapa, it's filled with tables at which sit sailors, drunk, bleary-eyed Gringos, with furtive playing-it-close Mexicans, groups of out-to-exploit, we-know-it-all men.

But there's a rather elegant visiting party of Gringos, the women wearing pastel shades of tricel. And there's a dance floor in between the tall bamboo tree-like posts which stretch up to the ceiling where hang perforated coconuts for lighting, the perforations coloured blue, pink, brown, mauve, yellow.

Here gathered round the bar at the entrance are the girls; some are undulating among the tables and others are sitting with their clients. One who is generously built and beautiful with dark, kind, motherly eyes has saucy great voluptuous breasts, drooping beneath her garments of hanging chiffon. Here is another girl whose breasts are laid out as if on a casserole, a sort of frilly shelf made from flounced silk. And there are sailors, bored sailors, sitting round everywhere in their floppy white uniforms with bottles of beer in front of them on the tables. They look too young to be sailors, some of them.

A sailor with an older more thoughtful face and a great spade of a beard has just come back with the flimsy girl he was with, a flimsy plump little girl in gold lamé trousers and a pink brassiere.

She escorts him back to his table and the other sailors don't look up as he sits down amongst them and he's trying to prolong that moment of tenderness. Give us a kiss, she kisses him on his hairy mouth, he taps her friendlily on the behind, Oh give us another kiss, and she is always friendly as if she'd like to stay. Finally she tears herself away and she's forgotten him as she steps out into the room again, looking around sexily, appraisingly, for new clients. There is also a girl who wears a flimsy see-through nightie and panties underneath but nothing over her breasts.

Those most mocked are the drunk Gringos because these are befriended by one or other of the frilly up-bosomed girls and before they know what is happening they find a girl sitting by them indeed almost on them, laughing in a sort of delighted complicity, great gusts and gales of laughter, and the massive form of the white-clad proprietor, his vast belly, his minute tin tray on which stands their order, his beer, her tiny glass of coloured water, his glassy grey eyes, his little moustache, his ferocious air of non-contact, and the girl is still gurgling and laughing, laughing with her delighted complicity.

The moment the drink has actually arrived, however, the smile mysteriously is gone from the girl's face and the steely-faced proprietor is demanding a huge price from him for the drinks. 'Oh no, that is too much,' blurts out the drunk American. But the words come out funny and the woman has now begun her over-whelming smiling and giggling again and he waggles his finger at the proprietor in a foppish manner and the proprietor angrily takes those same fingers in his iron paw and crushes them so the drunk decides that he had better pay up.

So he pays, and slowly the woman's face relapses into boredom as her drink gets lower in her glass and soon it will be time for him to buy her another. Certain Gringo men are the sad ones, those who don't know what they want. Did they come here for a drink or a girl or for the music or for what exactly? So while they try to puzzle it out they're fleeced.

Outside, amid the dust and the shacks of the freelances which span the dust-laden streets, there stands the home of the proprietor, a typical bourgeois home with spikes to protect it, steel sash windows, two floors, flowers, everything neat and tidy. You would think it stood beside a prosperous street except it doesn't. It stands amid a mud patch.

The tempo of the place is determined by the slow tides of man's lusts, the coming and going of girls and men, the girls walking proud, happy, unneurotic to their little houses, the men striding purposefully behind. Well, is having a girl the same as an expensive beer or different?

A man is tapping my shoulder. He opens a cigar box filled with something he wants to sell me. Authentic sacred American crosses.

Next morning I go out in a sailing boat into these famous blue waters and the scene is so perfect, so lyrical, that I lose track of time and though the rate is one peso a minute I let the minutes, the hours, drift away as we sail past the villas and past the palm-thatched hut where a Mexican pop group is playing Beatles numbers, and out onto the the pellucid blue water flanked on one side by a white sanded shore amidst the palm trees and on the other luxurious villas, hotels, stretching up floor after floor.

The girl takes off her bikini, there is little traffic on these waters, and her white breasts are covered by her long falling hair. The only passers-by are the steamers doing their guided tour of Acapulco and a water skier. A man also flips by in mid-air, hanging on to the end of a red and white striped parachute pulled by a boat, tossed up and down in the light buffeting winds.

And I think of a story, of an Englishman who is so enchanted with it all that he forgets his money situation, lets the hours, the days tick by. It is a hired boat, but for the moment he believes that it is his, and that he'll be able to live for ever in this enchantment.

15

The Highest High

It is not easy to taste the magic mushroom. For the foreigner searching through Mexico, even when he's bang on the track of it, it is as hard to taste this semi-religious substance as it would be for a Mexican Indian visiting a quiet British village, if he went to the vicar and told him that he had a desire to try some communion wine.

Also, not only local people, but governments too seem not to like the idea of strangers getting high on local concoctions. In Britain I remembered there are licensing laws.

It is the frightened denial of the possibility of ecstasy perhaps, this bloody saying goodbye to our Bacchic birthright in those chill desperate hours of the afternoon between three and five. Thus the British rulers (voted into power by British people) dictate about those substances we take into our bodies. Soon they'll start rationing women on making love. Although, in Indian territory, the police go no further in their jurisdiction than the boundaries of the Latinised towns, none the less in thousands and thousands of square miles of jungle and upland and forest, war appears to have been declared on the mushroom.

Through contact with various Americans, I was compiling a list of places where it was said that one could taste it. But such information was nearly always accompanied by this reservation; that my informants had heard that the police had been there since and had instructed the local populace to sell no more mushrooms to strangers.

Had it not been for the American girl; had it not been for a chance meeting on the slopes of Popocatepetl; had it not been for many things I might have left Mexico never having tasted the magic mushroom. In other places I have heard that the local priest has waged a relentless war against the mushrooms, feeling that, with their connections with older cults, they were a threat to Christianity. I was lucky.

There is a place where the shore stretches away in a series of lovely curves and along its banks are a number of long low shanties filled with bars, falling in a series of descending wooden floors, each brightly painted in crimson, amethyst, lemon-green, puce or whatever other unexpected colours of the rainbow you can think of.

Here shell food and sea food is sold, and here there are sailing boats of a tender gracefulness. Their masts are made from a single tall bamboo pole, their bodies are like cockle shells, and their sails are gently ribbed, and splashed with juicy colours as mouth-watering as water ices.

'Can you tell me where the magic mushrooms grow?' I ask an attendant. 'It is growing late in the year now, I would so like to be able to find some.'

The man acts as if he had not heard me. I repeat my question. And he says, 'Would you take me back to England? With you? Here is no good for me in this dead end place. Can you take me back with you?'

'But Acapulco is the best place in the world.'

'I desire so much to see those things that I have seen in the cinema. I have seen pictures of your cars and weddings. I have a motor bike?'

Ahead of us across the illimitable blue sea, boats are in full sail, tacking slowly out against the wind that blows in from the sea.

'I would like to see that place. Will you take me there?'

'But all I'd like to do is stay here for ever.'

'Well then we will do a swap,' he says, holding to me his tattered trouser leg, and indicating my elegant trousering.

I don't ask him again about the magic mushrooms. I know that he is considering my question, whether or not to answer it.

At length, clapping his hands, he orders another rum-filled coconut shell at my expense, and, when we are alone, says to me in an undertone, 'The magic mushrooms are for holy men, not for ordinary folk.'

'But I can take you to where the magic mushrooms grow,' said my girl. 'I didn't know you were interested in them. I didn't know that that was your reason for being in Mexico.'

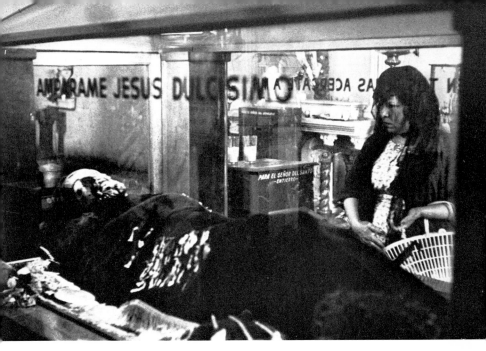

Outside a shrine

Indians in a trance-like state
inside one of their churches

Girls at a fiesta

Acapulco

'Nor did I,' said I. 'I didn't know till I got here, and even then I didn't know for a while, but now I know that that is why I came here.'

'Oh, well I've had them often. That's why I'm like I am.'

'Really?'

'There are many places where you can get the mushrooms but most of them are in Indian territory and it's dangerous to go there, or the police won't let you through, or both.

'I believe that you can get them up in the mountains round here. But I have no contacts here. The place where I got them is far away.'

'That's wonderful news,' I said. 'This explains something that I'd been wondering about you. Possibly through eating the mushrooms you have become different from other people. Certainly you seem different from other girls I've met.'

'It's possible.'

Feelings of being at the end of the world, and there is a powerful breeze raising old paper into the air as we finally reach a little square at the side of this remote mountain town.

We had been lurching over rough roads on the flanks of Popocatepetl until we reached a little village of similar seeming mud huts and went into the pulqueria and asked for a woman who we had been told could help us. At once everyone became excited and a number of people were offering to show us the way.

My girl was with me still. She told me that in this town, whose name was San Juan de la Mancha, she had heard that there might be mushrooms for sale in the market, or at any rate that the mushroom vendor there could tell us how to get to the purveyor of the mushrooms, Maria de los Hongos, and her priceless merchandise.

Now we were in a large red roofed plaster building redolent with the heady stench of Indians. 'You must refer to the mushrooms as "ninos",' said my girl. In a side stall, away from the main hall, sat an old man selling mushrooms. I asked him if he had any 'ninos' and a broad grin lit up his face. 'No,' he said, he didn't have any, but if we drove out of town, in a direction away from the main highway, we would see a dirt road on the left, not more than a quarter of a mile beyond the town. It was up this road that the village of San Juan de la Mancha was located.

E

We thanked him and drove off. We went out of the town about two miles, passing over a railroad crossing, searching scrupulously for a dirt road, but the sun was beginning to set and it was hard to see. We decided that we were lost. We tried again and discovered, some five hundred yards beyond the town, on our left, a widening in the road that appeared to lead into a field of cornstalks. This was our road. We travelled very slowly through the cornfields, the wheels lurching along through deep ruts in a very rocky dirt path. Once past the first field the road widened, the rocks became smaller and we began to climb up the side of the volcano. The road continued, slowly rising up the mountain, for a few miles. Then, suddenly, it made a sweeping turn, and we were driving into the town. San Juan de la Mancha consisted of not more than fifteen large red two-storey Indian huts and a sad red plaster church. These buildings were grouped around a square which in the waning light, looked as if it had never seen the shadow of a tree. It could have been a parched desert town from a Hollywood Western if it had not been for the mountain rising above us. There was a cantina, however. This solitary bar possessed the only light in town at that moment. We went inside. The cantina was barren inside except for a few cases of Cowenza and Coke and a pin-ball machine in the centre of the floor. Three Mexicans at this machine had stopped playing and were staring at us, possibly knowing why we were there. I asked for Maria de los Hongos.

'Ah, buscas a los ninos!'

I told him, yes, we were looking for the mushrooms. He asked us to follow him. As we stepped outside, an Indian woman, not very old, approached us and told us to come with her. The men from the cantina then left us.

The woman said that she was called Maria de los Hongos. She led us to a building at the far corner of the square, near the cantina, but at the opposite end of the square from the church. We went inside. It was a typical mud and plaster house, two-storied, with a large central courtyard. Sacks of grain were strewn about the floor. We walked upstairs behind Maria. Two other Indians had joined us and followed behind, one carrying a kerosene lamp.

On the upper storey were more sacks of grain, some opened to dry. Maria disappeared behind some sacks and shortly reappeared with a large cloth apparently filled with mushrooms. She opened the cloth and carefully spread the mushrooms out on it. She said that they had been freshly picked off the side of the mountain by some of the children in the village. She asked us, with a smile, if we liked what we saw, and when we said yes, asked if we wanted to try some.

'Yes.'

Maria counted out two dozen mushrooms carefully, and as she did so, muttered, 'So here they are, the little ninos.' She put them on a piece of newspaper.

'How many would you like?'

She counted out the mushrooms from the basket in twos, picking them up with her one hand and placing them in dishes, referring to each two that she picked up as if they were only one.

'*Que bellas ninos*!' she said. 'What beautiful children.'

Then she got a basin and placed it on the floor. She dabbled a flannel in the water in the basin and then wiped in turn our mouths, our chins, our foreheads, and eyes, and leaned towards us and whispered into each of our ears, very quietly, 'Don't tell anyone of this.'

We are sitting in a palapa near Acapulco. You can rent them for a few shillings a week. My girl has borrowed it from some American friends and now we are sitting in the interior, which is filled with a translucent golden light that pours through the bamboo branches of which it is made. A typewriter sits unexpectedly on the top of a table made from a single great chunk of wood.

She places the mushrooms in a bowl and holds the bowl over a low burning calor gas flame, and pours sugared water over the mushrooms.

'You must lie down,' she tells me, 'otherwise the effect may be too powerful.'

'Oh no – you do it first – you have first go. I want to watch you.'

She creeps about, panther-like, round the palapa, her hands clasped over the top of her head, sifting her mass of black hair.

I feel sick.

She says, 'I feel strange.'

'You can't yet.'

There is a pause, and she continues to stalk around. She stumbles over a cushion lying on the floor, shouts, 'Ih!'

She consults a large watch.

'Four minutes just coming up.' As the hand comes up to four minutes, she shouts, *'Quick I want to lie down! Quick!'*

I sit, watching her from the floor, hunched, with a sort of hatred. She falls onto the floor, flummoxes down, 'Oh! It's terrible! I'm going to die!'

A friend, an uncouth Mexican, watches intently. With a whisper she sinks back into what depths? She lies entirely still, moaning slightly.

'I'm all right,' she says, as I glance at her, concerned. 'I'll be silent for a bit now. Later I'll talk.'

She sits up and looks about her. She scrutinises me.

'You are a bird,' she says, 'a great dark bird. Haven't you got strange ears! They're like a bicycle! Oh, you're full of facts, completely, *pero completamente*, that's all there is inside you, fact after fact, you're stuffed with them, you're just a sackful of facts!'

'I'm not.'

'Yes you are, you bloody well are. Oh, aren't your hands extraordinary! Aren't they peculiar? You have extraordinary hands. Oh, but why are you so brave? I am. . . .' She stops, as if astonished, 'Oh, the *echo!* Oh, but why don't we *understand?* Now I see it, how is it I never knew, the echo, I've got it all straight at last, the echo is part of the. . . .'

Then suddenly she gasps, 'Oh. I didn't know you could see the sea from here.'

'Nor did I.'

'Oh, it's *coming!*'

'Where?'

'Well, there!'

'Oh, the sea's all around us! Oh bird, you seem so funny, sitting on your rock! No, but look, the sea! The sea!'

My girl has sunk back onto the floor. She whimpers, 'Now they're whispering, now they're muttering, now they're talking about me. And now it's the woman in blue. When I was a child they used to be like that, I used to creep round the house, I used to hear them discussing me, once my mother got twelve mind doctors and psychoanalysts to come to dinner and listen to me, and afterwards they were always plotting about me and talking about me, they said they were going to take me away. I think I'm going to die soon. I shall cry. Then they may love me. If I cry long enough they will love me.'

She catches sight of a huge piece of hardboard.

'What do you think of this picture?'

It is one of her daubs that she has made in the course of long summers in Mexico, a long procession of identical figures carrying torches, progressing along the side of a mountain towards a burning city. 'Oh, my *picture*! Oh, look at it! Oh, but I've only scratched it! There must be more! The sun must be more sun, and the moon must be more moon, and the world in the moon's face more dark and fast and the mountains must have light on them and the sky go more fast. . . . Oh, why can't we see, why can't we *see*! Oh, you're treating me like a child! Why can't we go to the sea? Why shouldn't we go to the sea? It's not far! It's only out there! Oh, you're treating me like a child! But it's you that are children.

'I think I'm going to die,' she says.

Then she springs to her feet, 'Hey, what's happened? You, you were there, now you're over there?'

I say, 'I moved.'

'Oh,' she says, scornfully. 'Is that all?'

On the floor our Mexican friend is reading a Mexican magazine, which shows a pin-up and proclaims, '*Mil ojos tiene la noche*'.

'Oh, it's cheap! It's cheap, it's dishonest! No one made this because they loved it, they made it because they wanted to make money!'

She takes the magazine and turns the pages to a headline saying, '*Los hippie hijos de Chappalla*'.

The girl, seeing the picture, shouts, 'It's wonderful! It's incredible! It's fantastic! Oh, why do I go on painting anyway, it's just so *useless*!'

Then the quality of the effect of the mushrooms on her seems to change. She raises her arm, announces, 'I want to make an announcement. . . . This is important. . . . Please write this down. . . . I am being born . . . it's all slime . . . all yellow . . . now it's all light! Oh help, now they're hitting me. . . . ! When I was living with Carlo he used to beat me, he used to whip me, I used to enjoy it, oh, why did I used to enjoy it so? Oh, this is extraordinary. . . . Oh, I must try not to hate men, try not to hate them or be frightened of them. Now I've realised something of immense importance. This is of fantastic importance. The woman in blue . . . the woman in blue . . . now I see it . . . the woman in blue, do you know who she was?'

She throws herself back, face down, on the mat on the floor.

'I've had asthma ever since then, ever since. Oh, I want to be loved. I want to cry so that I will be loved. She was – she was – the Virgin Mary!'

She rises and gazes at me.

'I love you.'

She puts her hand on mine and says, 'Spiritual love. Carnal love with this would be too much.'

Still with her painful eyes she gazes at me. 'Isn't it strange, I can look at you now, I wasn't able to look you in the eyes, but now I can.'

We go into a house on the edge of the town. We sit on the floor in the one large room before a small table behind which a magazine photograph of a Madonna is stuck over a nail. The old woman looks into each of our eyes, and sits down before us. My girl hands the mushrooms to the old woman, and she, in turn, takes a mushroom and places it inside our opened mouths. I believe she does not take any herself. She tells us to chew them carefully.

The mushrooms taste of the dirt that is clinging to them; however, they are not unpleasant. We chew slowly. There is a large pitcher of water to drink if we get thirsty. The mushrooms themselves are quite small with very thin long stalks. The largest of them have grey button tops about one inch and a half in diameter. My mouth is filled with a dry, typically mushroom-like taste.

The old woman lights an oil lamp and appears to be busy preparing some concoction from the mushrooms, although it might have been just something to eat.

I feel very anxious for something to happen. The house is very quiet, but outside there is a great deal of noise from what sounds like chirping crickets.

Half an hour passes before I become aware of the shadows against the wall that I am facing. They seem to be slowly moving and the colour of the wall has changed to a deep brown. I feel pleasant. As I stare at the wall my vision finally falls on the old woman. Her face seems to be moving, and composed of many more colours than I had noticed before. As I stare at her face, she seems to become a frog. Her whole person seems to grow into a frog-like being and her mouth begins to move. I remember staring at her mouth but being unable to make any sense of what she is saying. She isn't saying words to me, they are just sounds. I don't feel anxious about this, it seems all right not to make sense of her sounds.

Some time later I am staring pleasantly at the wall again, being preoccupied by the small roaches crawling along it and the cracks in it. I feel like an observer of some ancient civilisation. I see my girl beckoning me to a spot on the floor, she is intently watching three insects dragging a fourth across the floor.

I close my eyes and become involved in a fantasy that begins as bright clouds wandering through my mind, then it becomes shapes of chariots and castles that are constantly moving. There are glorious blue colours, more brilliant than those I normally dream. At one point I think I see a small boy by a ramshackle house, smiling and laughing. He has enormous black eyes.

I lose my sense of time; everything seems to be taking place in a way divorced from my normal manner of seeing things. I feel totally relaxed, at ease with my thoughts as well as my surroundings; a religious feeling. I open my eyes and the table before me and walls seem to shimmer; there is a bluish light over everything.

I eat more. They are horrible to eat – really horrible. I am pulling off bits of the slimy skin. I stuff the bits into my mouth. My gorge rises to meet them. I thrust some more of the mushrooms down my gullet. After a while comes an array of lights, lights of every colour and shifting pattern.

I feel as if a very heavy hand is pushing me down, down . . . my limbs feel heavy, I feel like one of those limp watches of Salvador Dali. Now I am borne on a fast moving, ever faster moving current of movement, and now comes a feeling of utter nausea. It is as if I stagger through pearls, caught in great shifting seas of coloured gems, coloured lights.

I am overwhelmed with laughter, then I go silent again. I feel a strong physical unease, as if by a change in my position I might make myself natural, comfortable. But I can't find that position. I say, 'I feel pretty bad now.'

A violent force seems to grip me and hurl me back onto the floor. My girl and the Mexican look over my way and exchange glances and I resent this. Now the sides of my vision become tinged, pinky green. I say, 'That frond of palm is a fantastic colour.' Time accelerates so that, when I next look up, I feel that ages have passed. My girl's eyes are dark pools of black, 'Oh, you look like a vampire, what has happened to you, have you put black on your eyes?'

I realise that she is talking with her friend and try to interrupt. I resent her having a conversation from which I am excluded. Again everything swoons around me, as if I am shooting along corridors of timelessness, then it is as if I am jerked abruptly to a halt. The words that she is saying seem malign and scornful. I say, stumblingly seeking for the words, 'Do you think that what you're saying is sense? It's not. . . .' After further waves wash over me I again hear them talking and say, 'Oh, I understand now, it's you that are having the conversation. I'm being ignored in it.' Fresh waves wash over me, then I come to and say, 'Oh! Here I am! I felt for a moment I was watching you through a wall, as if I was down here through a wall, in a coffin, watching you from a horizontal bunker of a green fish tank.'

Now again the clouds close in, with their multicoloured shades and prismatic colours, darkness swarms over me, there is complete darkness, then something makes me get up with a jerk, open my eyes, and I see a sight so fantastically funny that for days afterwards the sight keeps returning to me.

For my girl is rummaging behind a bead curtain. She produces a machete and waves it in the air and I go into fits of laughter, shouting; 'Funny, oh very funny! What a joke!' The image is so funny that for days after I laugh when I remember it. Everything seems to heave. The floor is fantastic now, writhing, wild, tawny, tossing its white blades, and the temptation comes to me, stand. I rise, with much searching and trying of my new limbs, and begin to walk round the room.

I have a great urge to go outside. I say, 'I must see the palm trees, let me.' I go out into the bathroom, peer across the terrace at the palm trees, and never have they seemed so green, so beautiful, so lovely. I run back, 'Come quick, come outside!'

I look through the door and see her, furtive, at the end of an illimitable corridor. I stand on the edge of the balcony, thinking; 'Space, *space*!' I am conscious of all things as they really are, untrimmed by the veil of seeing. Down in the jungle. Seeing the palm trees, I exclaim, 'Oh these, these are jokes!' The fronds are lush, intensely green, lush, dark, wonderful, watery. Just beyond the door to the palapa is shrouded with greenery, and beyond and above the trees are so immense, so high.

A little palm tree stands before me, I pluck a frond with its brilliant light green stalk and eat it. At once I begin to eat other things, grasses and leaves, all the wanton shrubbery, and seem to be joined with them now in a wonderful organic and vegetable unity. 'Look at this palm frond!' I pluck it, then thrust it in my mouth and munch it. Springing, feeling a new sensation of being in the free air or sky, I bound onto some stones, feel no pull of gravity, only stop for a moment to marvel at the fantastic wonderful shapes of the stones. Now everything seems very quiet and over one of the stones I peer at apparent deep, intense silence, a profound silence into which scatter the cold sparks of a man letting off fireworks, as if making stars amid the silence, as if this was the ultimate goal of all existence thus to make stars amid the silence. Behind him rise great buildings, noble, strange, sublime, wondrous against the light blue sky through the palm trees. To stand there is to see all things anew, as if peering through the branches of a mountain tree into a valley far below.

I return, leaping down from the stone heap. I see the wireless again, its interior seems to writhe, spindles, aluminium cogs and wheels, writhing and vibrating like terrible serpents. My girl is standing by the palapa door. I step down into the darkness. I climb up the springs of an old bed, and stand, creaking them. It seems that there is a veil between me and my girl, a thin dark-tinged veil, now I am overwhelmed with a feeling of love for her, uncloying my spirit, making me loving and free, irradiating in the cavern of my brain, lighting up the space behind my eyes. I stumble back through the darkness of the cavern, groping my way. At the top of the dark approach she stands, I climb up towards her, say, 'I come to tell you that I love you. . . .' My voice seems to echo across and across the space of the cavern. She laughs. There are gibberings and chitterings in the shadows. I lapse back into the cavern.

And now things appear to fly through the air, great tree trunks and boxes clatter about me. The Mexican runs down in to rescue me, and I feel his hands going over me, alarmed. He laughs. I mount from the cavern and join him. The first time, my girl had told me, you will be interested only in yourself. It's only after the third and fourth time that you will become aware of other people.

And indeed it is as if there is a purple veil drawn between me and them. My girl is squatting on the ground by a large metal object, and I squat down beside her. She ups her face at the sky. 'Oh Bird!' she cries. 'The insouciance! The gaiety! The tossing away! The abandon!'

'I resent that'

Again laughter doubles me up. I am convinced that she is joking.

'I resent that.'

Again I double up in laughter. She walks, upheaded, away. A stranger comes. I go to the corner of the palapa and peer out at him, scrutinising his face with fascination.

The trees outside the palapa once more intrigue me. They seem of immense height, fantastic. I look over among the trees, remark, 'Who could have told that sea filled all the forest?'

The ocean is running among the slow heaving trees. I look up at the sky and hold out my arms to swim into it. Trees are growing from the mound above the stones. Lightly I pull myself by the arms up the bending sapling. Lyrically, pliant footholds stretch themselves out sinuously for my feet. I climb into this world of green and yellow leaves and branches. The air, the warm balmy air, is an ocean in which I can swim. I am high now, high, and swimming through the sky. I climb higher among the swaying branches. I feel I have never known trees like this, these great toppling overhanging lovely palm branches. I pull at them, make them wave in the sky and the leaves toss and sway against the sky like the arms of a windmill. I am part of the trees, with them swaying, turning, in the darkening sky . . . and still at the end of the vista my girl sitting, earthbound, sitting hunched on the wall, seeming now insignificant yet still with this miraculous quality, but without dignity in herself, her body hunched up, her sad face shadowed purple under her hair. The man sitting beside her I am hardly conscious of, it is her I see as I sway back and forth at the top of my palm tree. I call out again, 'Who would have known that this place is all forest?' I call out to her to come and join me. Endless, without limit, the palm-trees stretch far away.

APPENDIX

Some Notes on the British Version of the Mushroom —
Amanita Muscaria

In *Wayside and Woodland Fungi* by W. P. K. Findlay, a charming
book which has some illustrations by Beatrix Potter, I read as
follows :

Amanita Muscaria: Fly Agaric (L. Musca Fly)
This most conspicuous fungus is a favourite subject for artists and
craftsmen, and frequently provides the stools for gnomes in children's
picture books. It is found in the autumn under birches, with the
roots of which it forms a mycorrhiza, or on poor soil round pine
trees. The cap, which may be as much as six to seven inches across,
is at first hemispherical, later becoming expanded and flattened. Its
typical rich scarlet colour may fade to orange or yellowish . . . . This
fungus is poisonous and it may cause violent intoxication, but is
seldom fatal. Infusions of the cap were once used to kill flies – hence
its name.

In *Common Edible Mushrooms* by Professor Clyden Christiansen,
who is professor of plant pathology at the University of Minnesota,
I read :

Poisonous: Amanita Muscaria (Fly Agaric)
The species' name is taken from the name of the common house
fly, *musca domestica*, because the fungus has a peculiar and fatal
attraction for the busy and annoying pests. If pieces of *A. Muscaria*
are broken up and placed in a shallow saucer of water, house flies
soon begin to cluster around, eager for a tipple. It is their last. In
a few moments, seemingly stimulated by this too potent elixir, they
take off and buzz about in frenzied loops and circles until sudden
death overtakes them, often in full flight, and they topple quite
lifeless to the floor. But flies are not the only creatures susceptible to
the peculiar attractions of this fungus, for in some regions of Siberia
it was once, and probably still is, commonly used as an intoxicant
by man, long lethal doses of it producing a temporarily glorious binge.
The after effects are less joyous, involving rather severe aches and

pains, but these do not seem to have deterred its use. *Eaten in quantity, of course, it is fatal.*

John Ramsbottom, in his book *Poisonous Fungi* states that the *Amanita* 'never causes death in healthy people'. He continues :

> Usually one to three hours or so after a meal of mushrooms there is a period of delirium and hallucinations, sometimes accompanied by intestinal disturbances. After a few hours this is followed by intense stupor and an awakening to complete forgetfulness. The fungus is eaten in some regions apparently without ill effect. The price in the barren steppes of Siberia is three or four reindeer for a single mushroom.

Mr Ramsbottom, who is Keeper of Botany in the Natural History Department in the British Museum, mentions also that it is common in woodlands and is scarlet once it has broken through its golden wall, remnants of which form its white or golden spots. It is to be found under oaks, birches, and pines.

The *Amanita* is reputed in Siberia to produce excessive emotion and also has been said to cause Viking warriors to go berserk.

A method of preparing Amanita Muscaria
The first thing is, identify your mushroom. A book on mushrooms should be carefully consulted. The mushroom's British growth period is from late August to October.

Then, so Colin Moorcroft writes in *Friends Magazine* (December 1970) :

> Gather twenty or so large fungi, and rinse to remove dirt. Cut the whole mushrooms into one cm. cubes, and spread out on a piece of aluminium foil or baking tray. Place in a ventilated oven, or home oven with the door ajar, and stabilise temperature at 250 degrees F. *Do not allow the temperature to exceed 290 degrees F.,* otherwise the hallucinogens evaporate. Cook until the fungus is brittle to the touch, i.e. will crumble to a fine powder when rubbed softly. This is normally about six hours, but varies with individual crops. Over-cooking does not harm anything, but undercooking does. Powder the fungus which may then be eaten, mixed into jam, in tea, or taken straight. Five level teaspoonfuls is a pleasant amount to take, although up to fifteen may be taken for special occasions. It is dangerous to exceed this dosage. Each mushroom reduces to about two level teaspoons of powder.

Those considering taking the mushroom themselves should bear in mind that it is often accompanied by extreme nausea, especially in the British versions. Think carefully before you take the plunge. This is important.

Lynn Darnton, in an article in *Oz* Magazine, has this to say about the preparation of the magic mushroom :

> When a mushroom field has been found one should arrange for them to be transported as quickly as possible to the place they are to be used, for they are very delicate plants. Ideally, they should be collected in large baskets during a fine morning, after the dew has risen but before the sun has had a chance to weaken their strength. Never fill baskets but always pack very loosely. It is an old law never to collect more than you yourself need, but if you wish to break this law, then they should be threaded together in such a way that they can be hung over a natural fire; not in the direct radiation, but over the warm (not hot) air currents rising from the fire. They should be left there for some fortnight or more till they are bone dry, and to accomplish this it is necessary to check them every day to ensure that none of the caps are touching under more than the slightest pressure, otherwise rot and maggots will quickly settle in. If this preparation is followed, the degree of nausea associated with eating fly agaric can be lessened although unfortunately not counteracted completely.

Here are accounts he gives of the ingestation of the two mushrooms – Psilocybe and Fly Agaric :

1 *Psilocybe*

Subject was at that time living in a small very old English village with a church and graveyard opposite his cottage. After collecting the mushrooms, he dried them slowly by the fire, ground them into a black powder, then ate them mixed with jam.

'Before the mixture had even entered my stomach I distinctly felt a pleasant electric shock shoot up from the base of my spine to the top of my head; as the initial tenseness subsided, my head began to tingle, and this tingling spread all over my scalp, slowly down across my forehead, followed by a sensation as if a white cloud quickly brushed across the surface of my eyeballs; the next moment the idea flashed across my mind : "My eyeballs have just been cleaned and see how new the world looks !" All this happened in perhaps two or three seconds. Moments later I was back in my familiar old room again, in a quite normal state of mind, wondering what on earth had happened a moment ago?

'Slowly I began to feel my body tingling, not a normal tingle but as if my body were "going away". I became claustrophobic and had to leave the house, so we both went together, and noticed, immediately we were outside, that the church was pointing the wrong way.

We went into the church to investigate and discovered that the ground plan was the reverse, longitudinally, of what it should be. We noticed that the floor was now lower than the original, and saw many ordinary and architectural details which only served to confirm our idea that the church was pointing the wrong way. . . .

'Some months later I discovered from a local farmer whose ancestors had lived at the farm for many centuries that the present church was built on the site of an earlier chapel, built on the site of an even earlier Celtic temple. . . .'

2 Fly Agaric

Subject found some fly agaric in a wild mountainous region and decided it must be the right time to eat some, for it was growing on the path. He partially dried it and ate it together with some special oils prepared to counteract the unpleasant sickness which might result from eating partially fresh mushrooms.

Initially there was a slow onset of nausea accompanied by a strong desire to vomit, although, having specially eaten nothing for a day or so, there was nothing in his stomach. The nausea developed to a most uncomfortable degree, but as the oils effectively counteracted this, he began to feel very happy.

'I was simply happy that everything was happening in such a beautiful way. Everything seemed to be essentially good, but as time passed I began to feel sad. I realised that I was seeing qualities of things I hadn't noticed before. Whenever I witnessed dishonesty, even to the slightest degree, my own dishonesty or that of others, I felt sick, yet when I witnessed creative and loving forces pass between people, I felt supremely happy. I understood dishonesty in a different sense from the normal; it was the refusal to understand, see, or acknowledge the obvious and as time passed everything became obvious.

'A single, pure, flute-like note played inside my head, and as I walked across the landscape this note changed. This I attributed to invisible energy permeating everything. I understood that everything has its particular note, or vibration which we can hear and feel if we become receptive. I heard choirs of angels and deities singing from the tops of hills, and each hill had its unique music; not music I can describe, for we do not have such music in our world; it was the music of living things, music of the trees and the sky, music of the wild animals, and so I realised that human music is usually a very poor attempt to communicate with living things or at least to reflect some of the qualities of living things. . . .'

On my return, for many months the mushroom eluded me in Britain as well. There, the presence of the British version (red with white spots) had been reported to me in woods in Wales near to where I often go. I searched and found, amid the boggy woodland, many types of mushroom and toadstool that I'd not seen before. Huge great hunks of khaki-coloured toadstool clung to the underside of vast beech boles. Then, marching along in their myriads, were an army of tiny little mushrooms, breaking out from a beech branch like a rash. Others, like huge loaves of bread, sat stolid amid the greenery.

At length, in woods owned by some Monmouthshire friends, I came upon the British version of the mushroom. Coyly hiding amid the brackenny undergrowth, the mushrooms sat, their heads slightly breasting the crisscross of dead leaves and twigs above them.

I took them with me, wrapped them in silver paper, and put them in my refrigerator. Later, I came back and found that they had shrunk out of all recognition. Fool that I was, I threw them away. How crazy can you get? Of course the magic must still have been in them.

SELECTED BIBLIOGRAPHY

Allegro, John M., *The Sacred Mushroom and the Cross*, London: Hodder & Stoughton, 1970.

Castaneda, Carlos, *The Teachings of Don Juan: A Yaqui Way of Knowledge*, Harmondsworth, Middlesex: Penguin Books, 1970.

Chadbourne, Marc, *Anahuac*, London: Elek Books, 1954.

Barnton, Lynn, 'O Magik Mushroom', *Oz* Magazine, 31, 1970.

Findlay, W. P. K., *Wayside and Woodland Fungi*, London: Frederick Warne, 1967.

Graves, Robert, 'Jesus as Toadstool', *New Statesman,* 1970.

—— 'What the Gods Turned On On', *Queen* Magazine, 1970.

Heim, R., and Wasson, R. G., 'Les Champignons Hallucinogènes du Mexique', Musée National d'Histoire Naturelle, 1957.

Moorcraft, Colin, 'Amanita Muscaria', *Frendz* Magazine, 1970.

Puharich, Andrija, *The Sacred Mushroom*, London: Victor Gollancz, 1959.

Ramsbottom, John, *Poisonous Fungi,* Harmondsworth, Middlesex: Penguin Books, 1945.

Schultes, Richard Evans, Lectures to the College of Pharmacy, University of Texas, *The Psychedelic Reader* and *Texas Journal of Pharmacy,* 1961.

Simon, Kate, *México: Places and Pleasures*, New York: Doubleday, Dolphin Books, 1963.

Taylor, N., *Flight from Reality*, New York: Dell, Sloan & Pearce, 1949.

Wasson, R. G., Lecture to the Mycological Society of America, *The Psychedelic Reader* and Botanical Museum Leaflet 19(7), Harvard University, 1961.

Wasson, R. G., and Wasson, V. P., *Mushrooms, Russia and History*, New York: Pantheon Books, 1957.

Weil, M. Metzner, R., and Leary, T. (eds), *Psychedelic Experience*, New York: University Books, 1964.